No Excuses: Coaching High School Cross Country (revised)

John Wesley Slider

DEDICATION

This book is dedicated to my wife, Lillian, our daughter, Heather, and our son, William. It is also dedicated to the many athletes that I coached.

CONTENTS

INTRODUCTION

Though information contained in this book covers my entire Cross Country coaching career at two schools (2001-2006), the core of this book is a chronicle of what was a special season for a special group of runners – the J. Graham Brown School 2004 Cross Country team. It also may provide some modest coaching tips for anyone who desires to work with Cross Country runners.

This book is personal for several reasons. Coaching is personal. It involves the whole person. Coaching is based on a relationship with athletes, parents, teachers, and others. Cross Country especially creates the opportunity for a coach to influence positively the lives of young athletes.

The 2004 team at J. Graham Brown School was personal to me because of the runners on the team. I coached many of them for four years and more. It was personal because my son's last high school Cross Country season was the 2004 season. Because it is personal, this book is written with a personal voice.

This book is not about me, the coach, but about the runners. I need to start somewhere – with someone – however, and it is easier to begin the story with me.

Lillian, my wife, and I were very pleased that our son, William, was admitted to The J. Graham Brown School as a freshman. He entered the school as a member of the Class of 2005.

Brown provided, we believe, an environment in which William matured and excelled academically, athletically, emotionally, and socially. We were very pleased with the school.

William was very excited to begin Cross Country at Brown in 2001. He knew the coach and another runner at Brown, Rob Halsell (Class of 2004). Rob and William got to know one another when they ran on a club team that went to the AAU nationals the year before (finishing tenth in the nation). On the long trip to the meet in Joplin, Missouri, Rob talked to Will about Brown School.

I learned a lot about the school on the trip from Rob's father – also Rob Halsell (I called him "Chief" – he was in the Navy – or "Deacon" – he was a Baptist Deacon). Joplin is eleven hours one-way, and "The Chief" and I sat together on the team bus – all the way there, and all the way back.

About five days before the start of Cross Country practice for Brown on July 15, 2001, I called the school office in order to contact the Cross Country coach and see what we needed to do for William to begin with the team. I was given the coach's telephone number.

I immediately called the coach. He told me right away that he was considering resigning as coach and returning to his home in Ashland,

Kentucky. I quickly found the school's telephone number again, and called again. The line was busy.

I waited ten minutes and called again. The secretary, Mary Leonard answered and I told her that I had just called about Cross Country. She said, "What a coincidence! The coach just called and resigned!"

I asked if I could speak with the Director of Athletics, Marcia Morton. I apologized to her, rather sheepishly. I did not intend to be the catalyst for the coach's resignation.

In the course of my conversation with Marcia, I offered to get the team going and coach until she found someone qualified. Apparently, she never did, because I coached five Cross Country and Track seasons and four Swimming seasons at Brown![1]

At the end of the 2006 Track season, I realized that I needed a change in coaching venues. Mr. Robert Vinegar, the Director of Athletics at Shawnee High School, gave me the opportunity to coach Cross Country at his school. I accepted this position, believing that I could survey the area and school for possible ministry opportunities for the United Methodist Church.

I found many opportunities for ministry. I was even offered a teaching position at Shawnee High School. At the end of the 2006/7 academic year I had to make a decision, however, based on both family and professional factors. I decided to accept an appointment within the United Methodist Church in June 2007 that I believed would allow me to reshape the way in which the United Methodist Church was in ministry in the Louisville community. I would not have time to coach. I, therefore, ended my coaching career with the Track season of 2007.

---

[1] I did not come totally unqualified. I already had my certification from the KHSAA and had coached basketball, soccer, softball, and volleyball.

1 WE ARE CREATED TO RUN

"I can't run!" How many times have I heard that!? – usually in a whinny voice.

"Wait a minute," I say. "Let me give you the running test." That usually gets the student curious.

"First, stand in front of me with both hands at your side. Now put one foot forward. Now put the other foot forward. See, you can run!"

Running comes naturally to humans – especially middle and high school students. We are created to run.

The Physiological Aspects of Running

You and I need the activity of running in order to be healthy. For example, human bones become brittle and weak if they are not stressed daily. In contrast, animals that are designed to hibernate up to six months out of the year experience no bone deterioration with inactivity.[2]

Other studies suggest there are physiological benefits from running. Barry L. Jacobs of Princeton compared the brains of mice that ran everyday on an exercise wheel to the brains of mice that were sedentary. The active mice developed more brain cells and learned faster.[3]

Certainly, running is physiologically stressful. Running is too stressful only to a person who is not accustomed to running. With training running becomes normal. It is already natural.[4]

Children enjoy running. They are better equipped physiologically to run than adults. Young girls can run as easily as young boys.[5]

---

[2] Bernd Heinrich, *Why We Run*, p201.
[3] Bernd Heinrich, *Why We Run*, p234.
[4] Bernd Heinrich, *Why We Run*, p234.

The Cardio-Vascular System. The key to distance running is supplying fat-burning muscles with a sustained supply of oxygen. The complex system that supplies oxygen to the muscles requires a large heart with a large stroke volume per beat, a heart that is able to beat rapidly and slowly as needed, large arteries, extensively developed capillaries, a large lung capacity, large fuel deposits, and cells that are packed with mitochondria to convert (metabolize) fuel and oxygen into energy.[6] Essentially, your body runs like a car engine. Oxygen + Fuel = Energy.

Most people take in more oxygen than they can use because of inefficient blood flow from the heart.[7] The cardio-vascular system can be trained to function more powerfully and efficiently. The maximum volume of oxygen a person can process on a sustained and steady basis is the person's maximal aerobic power and is symbolized by the formula VO_2 *max*.[8]

An important distinction is the way energy is produced in the body. Aerobic energy production uses oxygen to burn the fuel for energy. Anaerobic energy production does not need oxygen.

Sprinters, jumpers, and throwers in track require high bursts of energy rather than sustained periods of (relatively) low energy. The shorter the distance and the more explosive the event, the more anaerobic power and the less aerobic power is required.

A sprinter, therefore, who has covered 200m at maximum speed, more than likely is breathing harder after his race than a middle distance runner who has completed 1600m at maximum pace. Of course, a middle distance or distance runner who "kicks" at the end of the race is actually dipping into anaerobic power and will, therefore, exhibit hard breathing.

The sprinter has used predominately anaerobic power, lactic acid has quickly collected in his muscles, and he requires extra oxygen to oxidize the lactic acid. The distance runner has use predominately aerobic power and has oxidized his lactic acid during the race. Depending on the athlete the need for a balance of anaerobic and aerobic power occurs in runs of 600m to 800m.

Cool muscles unload oxygen from the blood more slowly than warm muscles. A cool muscle has a reduced capacity for higher rates of output.[9] A good warm up not only heats the muscles, it prepares the body for aerobic metabolism.

---

[5] Arthur Lydiard, *Distance Training for Young Athletes*, p10.
[6] Bernd Heinrich, *Why We Run*, p65.
[7] Arthur Lydiard, *Distance Training for Young Athletes*, p20.
[8] Bernd Heinrich, *Why We Run*, p69. Larry Greene, *Training Young Distance Runners*, p37.
[9] Bernd Heinrich, *Why We Run*, p20. Arthur Lydiard, *Distance Training for Young Athletes*, p34.

Breathing requires energy. This thought seems insignificant until you realize that in a 5K race you will probably inhale or exhale at least 1,500 times. Breathing efficiency is, therefore, important and is increased by synchronizing the breathing cycle to the stride and by improving the depth of breathing.[10]

In my own experience, I learned to breathe in cycle with my running when I moved from the short sprints to the long sprints in college. I began working out with a swimmer who suggested that I learn to breathe in rhythm with my strides. For a 400m race I would run the first 200m inhaling then exhaling when my left foot struck the track. At the 200m mark I would increase my breathing rhythm – inhaling on the left foot strike and exhaling on the right. I felt that the coordination of breathing a stride created a smoother run and gave me a boost at the right time.

Muscles. You have in your body a mixture of what are called fast-twitch (white meat) and slow-twitch (red meat) muscles. Your muscles throughout your body are, therefore, various shades of pink. Fast-twitch muscles provide powerful contractions for sprints. Slow-twitch muscles are suited for endurance runs. It is not known if your mix of muscles was predetermined at birth or fixed at a certain age because of lifestyle.

Fast-twitch (anaerobic) muscles do not require oxygen to produce energy. They work without oxygen to burn carbohydrates for explosive bursts of energy. Slow-twitch (aerobic) muscles do require a continuous supply of oxygen. Elite distance runners have a muscle mix containing 79% to 95% slow-twitch. Elite sprinters have about 25% slow-twitch. It is assumed that the average person has 50% slow-twitch.

There are two types of fast-twitch muscles – "A" and "B." Fast-twitch "A" muscles are anaerobic but can be trained to perform aerobically. The average person has 50% ST, 25% FTA, and 25% FTB.[11]

This proportion of muscle fibers suggests the importance of individual choice. If we assume every runner starts with the average distribution of muscle fibers (ST, FTA, FTB), then every runner (on average) can train 75% of his or her muscles to perform aerobically.

For example, my son William and I are built to be sprinters. We have large thigh muscles, and – we assume – have predominantly fast twitch or "sprinter's" muscles. Yet, William, though he was a good long sprinter and intermediate hurdler in high school, preferred Cross Country and with training became a capable high school and college distance runner. I never raced more than 400m in college, but during my Marine Corps career I converted to distance running with modest success.[12]

---

[10] Bernd Heinrich, *Why We Run*, p227.

[11] Bernd Heinrich, *Why We Run*, pp65ff.

[12] Coincidentally, William and I have personal best times in the 5K/3 mile run with ten seconds of each other.

There is a cost, of course. The cost of aerobic running fitness is a loss of explosive muscular strength or sprint speed.[13] This loss can be reversed, however, by a shift in training. A 400m runner, therefore, should not fear training aerobically during Cross Country. With an appropriate transition period speed can be regained and the cardiovascular base work accomplished during Cross Country season is retained.

It has already been noted that there is a wide range of muscle fiber distribution from individual to individual. That is why some runners are sprinters and others are ultra marathoners. There are also differences of fiber distribution within individual bodies. In addition, there may be differences in muscle fiber distribution between sexes.

For example, the male bullfrog has fast-twitch muscle fibers in his leg muscles designed to perform anaerobically for an explosive release of energy. The female bullfrog shares the leg design of the male bullfrog.

Male bullfrogs are also skilled in endurance shouting (croaking). Their chest muscles perform aerobically. Female bullfrogs are not endurance shouters and their chest muscles have significantly fewer slow-twitch fibers.[14]

Again, our son, William, exhibits a difference in types of muscles within his body. While his legs appear to be predominantly fast twitch that he trained to function as slow twitch, his upper body seems to be predominantly slow twitch. In running he was a long sprinter who made himself a distance runner. In high school and college he was a distance swimmer.

Elimination of Waste. A car produces energy by burning fuel and oxygen. Waste, in the form of exhaust is also produced. Your body processes and eliminates metabolic waste through the kidneys and liver.[15]

Bipedal Running and Heat Dissipation. Bipedal animals are two-legged runners who run by a succession of long leaps, either one leg in alternation, or both legs together.[16] Bipedal running is less efficient that quadrupal (four legged) running in that it consumes more energy.[17]

Bipedal running does have an advantage. It is more efficient in thermoregulation – the dissipation of heat. Bipedal animals have 60% less exposure to solar radiation. In addition, bipedal animals have better convective cooling systems.[18] An erect posture coupled with the hairless bodies of humans increases the area of exposed skin for cooling.[19]

---

[13] Bernd Heinrich, *Why We Run*, p201.
[14] Bernd Heinrich, *Why We Run*, pp144ff.
[15] Bernd Heinrich, *Why We Run*, p69.
[16] Bernd Heinrich, *Why We Run*, p158.
[17] Bernd Heinrich, *Why We Run*, p165.
[18] Bernd Heinrich, *Why We Run*, p166.
[19] Bernd Heinrich, *Why We Run*, pp172f.

Dissipation of internally generated heat is one of the most potent factors limiting endurance.[20] In addition to the enhanced convective cooling provided by erect stance and hairless bodies, humans also have well-developed sweat glands that allow humans to tolerate very high heat loads. The cost is water loss.[21] Finally, the human brain has a network of veins that act as a radiator to combat the effect of solar radiation on the most sensitive organ in the human body.[22]

Proper Running Form. Proper running form minimizes inefficient motion and decreases wasted energy. A 5K race takes as many as 6,000 steps, depending on the speed and height of the runner. The energy cost for these 6,000 steps for a 150 pound runner is 300 kilocalories. You save energy through lessening the weight of your feet and through good mechanics that minimize up and down motion.[23] Energy must be expended as much as possible toward horizontal motion, not vertical or lateral. What a distance runner can least afford is lifting the entire body with each step.[24]

Distance running form seeks to save energy. It is different from sprinting form because sprinters are not concerned with saving energy, but with rapid foot turnover. A sprinter will seek to lessen the weight of his or her foot in order to move the foot forward through the long stride. To lengthen the stride and "lighten" the foot sprinters develop high knee action and bring the foot up almost to the hip or thigh in the recovery.[25] Raising the foot in the recovery even slightly will lessen the energy required to move the foot forward. What the distance runner must remember is that it also takes energy to lift the foot.

In bipedal runners there is a heavy impact on each foot with every step.[26] Each foot strike loses energy. The loss of energy through the impact of the foot is minimized by the stretching of the heel (Achilles) tendon on impact and contracting on impact. This tendon can store up to 40% of the energy of

---

[20] Bernd Heinrich, *Why We Run*, p171.

[21] Bernd Heinrich, *Why We Run*, p174.

[22] Bernd Heinrich, *Why We Run*, p173.

[23] Bernd Heinrich, *Why We Run*, p225.

[24] Bernd Heinrich, *Why We Run*, p227.

[25] Bernd Heinrich, *Why We Run*, p225.

[26] There have been some interesting developments recently with shoeless running. I became aware of these developments after this book was written. Shoeless running is a new area of investigation that may prove beneficial to distance runners by lessening the impact of the foot strike. Shoeless running causes the runner to strike the surface not with the heel but toward the ball of the foot. The force of the impact is lessened significantly. There are now products available that provide the effect of shoeless running without using bare feet.

the impact.[27] The stretching and contraction of this tendon and connected muscles is sometimes called ankle flip. The arch of the foot also stores energy and the combination of the arch and heel tendon can return almost 70% of the energy of the impact.[28]

Barefoot running can also be a means of lightening the foot, but a good shoe can also store and return energy. The combination of advanced track surfaces and shoe construction and heel tendon and arch will return up to 90% of energy stored from impact.[29]

Whether you are a sprinter or distance runner, your foot should strike the ground in a line below the knee and hip. If your foot strikes the ground ahead of your knee your foot will act as a brake. For distance running your foot should plant straight on the heel and roll slightly on the outside of the front of the foot. Running on the outside of the foot is called pronation. Slight pronation is appropriate. Excessive pronation will cause injuries as will excessive suppination (running on the inside of the foot).[30] A good running shoe salesperson or coach will spot these problems. Shoes can compensate for pronation or suppination.

You should think "straight and relaxed" in your running form. Arms should move straight and not be drawn across the chest. Higher arm action is required for sprinting. Clinched fists add to strain and do not increase speed.[31] The upper body should be relaxed and held upright over the hips with the shoulders square and the head level.

Contra-rotation (twisting) of the trunk should be kept to a minimum. Excessive contra-rotation of the upper body drains energy.[32]

Information for Girls. There is a statistical male running advantage over females. This advantage may relate to differences in hip structure, weight distribution, and foot length.[33] A statistical advantage does not dictate an individual advantage. Many females, especially young girls, can out run their male counterparts. Only elite male runners can out run elite female runners.

Girls, as you mature, your hips will widen, your weight distribution will change, and you *may* lose some ability to run at the level you did when you were younger. This possible loss will be caused by your change in running form (you will carry your arms higher across your chest to compensate for the changed weight distribution, and your legs will not move through or straight

---

[27] Bernd Heinrich, *Why We Run*, p158. Arthur Lydiard, *Distance Training for Young Athletes*, p38.

[28] Bernd Heinrich, *Why We Run*, p158.

[29] Bernd Heinrich, *Why We Run*, pp158f.

[30] Larry Greene, *Training Young Distance Runners*, p64.

[31] Peter Coe, *Winning Running*, p53.

[32] Peter Coe, *Winning Running*, p53.

[33] Bernd Heinrich, *Why We Run*, p132.

forward because of your widened hips).[34] The important word here is **MAY!** Mature women have more subcutaneous fat in their muscles than men, and this is an advantage in endurance running.[35]

Women who run distances at the elite level do so at a reproductive cost. They lose so much body fat that ovulation ceases.[36] The cessation of ovulation, if it occurs in you, is not something to be feared. It is not permanent, and the mileage you will run at middle school or high school will not cause any damage.

An average girl will begin her growth spurt at ten and one-half years. The growth spurt typically peaks at eleven or twelve. Menarche, the onset of menstruation, will occur at about twelve and one-half years or later.[37] You and your parents should be the judge as to whether to run on a particular day. I have a daughter who was very active athletically and I am aware of these issues.

Girls will hit their peak physical strength around fifteen or sixteen.[38] Between eleven and fourteen, young women will experience many changes. The long bones in your arms and legs will grow, which may create a tendency toward poor posture. Your height and weight will increase and your heart size will increase, causing your endurance to possibly be reduced. The mechanics of your running may change.[39] Again, do not fear this change. Many girls, obviously, are well-suited to continue running during and after these changes.

Forty years ago there were very few competitive female distance runners.[40] It is difficult to predict, therefore, if the female statistical disadvantage will remain, or if females will surpass males. The male statistical advantage may well be due to cultural, societal, and numerical factors rather than physical.

As an observation, you can look at high school swimming. Swimming has been a sport where girls have competed as long as boys. In most states, including Kentucky, there are twice as many girls swimming in high school as there are boys. Females statistically dominate the distance event (500y freestyle – this is the longest swim in high school and is equivalent to a 2000m run. It is not, therefore, truly an endurance swim). The top boys still beat the top girls, but not by much. The tenth place girl's time in the 500y freestyle is better than the tenth place boy's time. This statistical dominance

---

[34] Arthur Lydiard, *Distance Training for Young Athletes*, pp10f.

[35] Arthur Lydiard, *Distance Training for Young Athletes*, p11.

[36] Bernd Heinrich, *Why We Run*, p118.

[37] Larry Greene, *Training Young Distance Runners*, p7.

[38] Larry Greene, Training Young Distance Runners, p17.

[39] Arthur Lydiard, *Distance Training for Young Athletes*, p16.

[40] Bernd Heinrich, *Why We Run*, p131.

may be due to an interweaving of several factors – fewer cultural and social barriers to females swimming, the numerical advantage of females, higher body fat in females making them lighter in the water, and the elimination of leg and foot power and length as a factor.

Information for Boys. On average boys begin their growth spurt at age twelve and one-half and hit their growth spurt peak at age thirteen and one-half to fourteen.[41] Boys, you need to realize, therefore, that your physical growth is on average two years behind girls. If you start running at a young age you must be prepared emotionally to be beaten early on by girls.

In addition middle school boys will not find it as easy to compete against high school boys as middle school girls compete against high school girls. We had that situation at Brown School where two eighth grade girls, Kelly McRoberts and Maddie Dailey, found success at a young age against high school runners, whereas most of their male contemporaries had to wait a couple of years to be individually competitive against high school runners.

Boys, you will also need to be prepared for a big growth spurt around the eighth grade. This period is when William, our son, grew four inches and forty pounds in one year. In seventh grade he competed at the national level in Cross Country. His eighth grade year was one of transition as he got used to his new body and grew into a long sprinter. We simply built on his distance base, reorganized his training, and moved into different events.

Diet. Elite runners have special items in their diets that they believe helps them perform at the highest levels. Hicham Guerrouj of Morocco, who held the 1500m world record and was the 2000 Olympic silver medalist in that event, consumes a carbohydrate rich food, called *coucous.*[42] Lasse Viren of Finland, who won four Olympic Gold medals at the 5,000m and 10,000m in 1972 and 1976, credits reindeer milk that is rich in protein and fat.[43] Naoko Takahshi, an elite female marathoner from Japan who won the 2000 Olympic marathon, drinks the stomach secretions of the larval grubs of giant killer hornets.[44]

Really, the best advice is to eat what you feel like eating provided the food is fresh, wholesome, and nourishing.[45] Your body will tell you what it

---

[41] Larry Greene, *Training Young Distance Runners*, p7.

[42] Bernd Heinrich, *Why We Run*, p213.

[43] Bernd Heinrich, *Why We Run*, p214.

[44] Bernd Heinrich, *Why We Run*, p216. This drink of choice originates as an insect that an adult giant killer hornet has caught and eaten. The digested material is regurgitated and fed to the grubs (babies) who in response vomit up clear liquid droplets. Takahshi would drink the clear liquid. This concoction makes my honey and peanut butter sandwiches before high school meets seem tame, until I realized that honey is simply a bee regurgitate!

[45] Arthur Lydiard, *Distance Training for Young Athletes*, p49.

needs and will choose appropriately – provided the choices are nutritional and minimally processed.[46] If nutrients are lacking in the food we eat – if our calories are empty – our bodies will tell us to continue eating. The result is weight gain.[47]

Different foods for training and racing are not required for races of twenty to thirty minutes or less.[48] For a 5k race you should have enough carbohydrates stored in your body to sustain maximum work output.[49] Some of our training runs at Brown School that were over thirty minutes caused runners to dip into fat stores. During this shift from carbohydrate to fat you may experience what is called a "runner's high." If there is not enough fat in your body to sustain you in these runs, protein (muscles and organs) is consumed.[50]

Runners should not try to diet, but simply eat healthy foods. In animals that live where food is continually available, there is no need to store fat. Animals who live in environments where the food supply is seasonal and/or who hibernate, food is stored as fat. Human bodies are designed to store fat, but our contemporary environment has made food continually available.[51]

Some runners try to lose weight by drastically cutting food consumption or fasting. These strategies, however, signal the body to shut down because food is becoming scarce. Mobility is reduced, food is converted into fat, and metabolism is slowed.[52] Dieting can reduce the metabolic rate by almost half, making the person weak, sluggish, and slow, while reducing weight only slightly.[53] It is best to allow your body to find its own weight through activity and gradual decrease in consumption.

Many high school girls become too concerned with how they look and begin to diet at early ages. While there is certainly a concern now days for teen-age obesity, this problem should be addressed through increased activity rather than decreased eating.

Our daughter, Heather, was a four sport, year-round athlete in high school and an NCAA division I athlete in college. Lillian, my wife, discouraged any dieting by Heather in middle school or high school. Heather

---

[46] The hypothalamus regulates basic food requirements for the body, but the mind can control the hypothalamus. Anorexia is evidence of the mind controlling the hypothalamus. Bernd Heinrich, *Why We Run*, p207.

[47] Bernd Heinrich, *Why We Run*, p208.

[48] Bernd Heinrich, *Why We Run*, p212.

[49] Bernd Heinrich, *Why We Run*, p223.

[50] The protein that is consumed in starvation situations is the bodies own organs and muscles.

[51] Bernd Heinrich, *Why We Run*, p202.

[52] Bernd Heinrich, *Why We Run*, p202.

[53] Bernd Heinrich, *Why We Run*, p206.

ate what she wanted at school and at home, while other girls her age were dieting. When she went to college she did not put on the "freshman fifteen" that many girls seem to gain. She is now in her early thirties and has always had an attractive, slender, athletic build.

Females on average have more body fat and store and retain fat more easily than males. Females need fat stores for pregnancy and lactation.[54]

I do not encourage gimmicks and additives. High fat diets will not help runners in events 5K or below.[55] A vitamin and mineral supplement is fine. Alcohol has no positive role in the runner's diet.[56] "Defizzed" cola is about the best drink for a pre-race boost if needed.

For races under 5K it is probably best not to eat prior to the event. Runners at the high school distances must train their digestive system to shut off for racing.[57] As a long sprinter in college I would always want to run hungry. I would never eat less than 4 hours before a race.

There is the true story of two Brown School runners who went to the Dairy Queen for an ice cream cone prior to a race at Seneca Park. They ran the entire race with "intestinal trauma," crossed the finish line, and headed straight for the restrooms. They will go unnamed, but they are legends.

Another unnamed runner had not properly "prepared" for the regional championship race, and had to make a mid-course adjustment into the woods. I called him Chief Poopindawoods.

The Psychological Aspects of Running

The psychological aspects of running should not be minimized. The will to succeed in some respects involves self-delusion. You have to fool yourself to go beyond your current limits.

Achievement in running, however, must be based on a realistic assessment of your capabilities coupled with your dreams. Courage is the bridge between capabilities and dreams.[58] Courage should be recognized wherever it occurs, and for some it some takes courage just to stay with the pack.

One of the advantages of bipedal running is the ability to see beyond the immediate to the goal or dream. The body can only reach the next step, but the mind can reach to the next hill, and the next, and the next....

Kenyan athletes have recently realized great successes in running. What can explain the Kenyan success story?

---

[54] Bernd Heinrich, *Why We Run*, p204.
[55] Larry Greene, *Training Young Distance Runners*, p21.
[56] Peter Coe, *Winning Running*, p16.
[57] Bernd Heinrich, *Why We Run*, p223.
[58] Bernd Heinrich, *Why We Run*, p197.

The top Kenyan runners come from one locality and one specific group – the Kalenjin – and specifically, one subgroup – the Nandi. The Nandi of Kenya are known to be quiet, ascetic, serious, hardworking individualists who are oriented toward high achievement. Their traditional "sport" was cattle raiding.[59] Culturally, they value and admire the best runners. Nandi children want to be good runners. They succeed at running because they want to succeed.

Primitive cats and dogs both had to hunt to survive. Most no longer need to do so, but they have both kept their primitive inclinations about running. Cats will run only if they have to run – to eat or for protection. Dogs love to run. They have a desire to run.

There has never been a cat as a part of the sled team in the Iditarod race. Only dogs pull the sleds in that endurance race in Alaska. Iditarod dogs are selected for their strong appetite, deep chest, strong cardiovascular system, and (most important) their desire to run.[60]

Here are some thoughts about the psychological aspects of running:

"You must be a little crazy."[61]
-Don Ritchie, ultra marathoner, Great Britain

"The will to win means nothing without the will to prepare."[62]
-Juma Ikangaa, marathoner, Tanzania

"In athletics it is culture and not biology, attitude and not altitude, nurture and not nature, which are crucial variables which explain individual athletic success…."[63]
- John Bale and Joe Sang

"The idea of talent is only a myth because talent is only manifest in retrospect. The myth should be smashed, toppled because it is an insult to consider an athlete who made it to the top, unfairly and inevitably because of his or her genes, and not because the athlete decided by thinking in an act of free will to try to win…. The talent lies not in our genes, but in our minds."[64]
- Tom Derderian

---

[59] Bernd Heinrich, *Why We Run*, p193.
[60] Bernd Heinrich, *Why We Run*, pp189f.
[61] Bernd Heinrich, *Why We Run*, p224.
[62] Bernd Heinrich, *Why We Run*, p221.
[63] Bernd Heinrich, *Why We Run*, p195.
[64] Bernd Heinrich, *Why We Run*, pp195f.

"If you don't stop running, I'm going to have to take that knee cap off and throw it in the garbage can."[65]
-Orthopedic surgeon to Bernd Heinrick, several years before his 1981 100K world championship

"Now if you are going to win the battle, you have to do one thing. You have to make the mind run the body. Never let the body tell the mind what to do. The body will always give up."[66]
- General George S. Patton, 1912 U.S. Olympic Team

"It's ninety percent mental. The other half is physical."[67]
-Yogi Berra, baseball player

The Anthropological Aspects of Running

The Cross Country race is a reenactment of the primitive communal hunt. We were created to run for the purpose of hunting. We are descended from the best hunters and runners - those who survived by running to hunt. Survival meant continual activity, and those who were capable of such activity survived.

Primitive humans did more than just run. They were long distance hunters because they could not out sprint their prey. Humans are better suited physically and psychologically for long-range hunting. Physically, we are more able to run in the heat of the day than our prey. Psychologically, we learned to dream and to have long-range goals.[68] Long distance hunting requires the ability to dream and project yourself into the future.

The Khoisan of South Africa and the Tarahumara of Mexico still today are known to run their prey – exhausting the hunted animal – provided they can do it during the heat of the day.[69]

Since primitive humans were hunters who could not individually out run their prey, they developed social skills. They hunted together as a team.[70] They resembled dogs by hunting in packs over long distances, rather than cats that hunt alone with a sudden pounce or burst of speed.

Some have suggested that the differences in athletic performance between males and females originate in the division of labor in primitive society. Males hunted (ran). Females foraged, cared for the young, and chose

[65] Bernd Heinrich, *Why We Run*, p255.
[66] Bernd Heinrich, *Why We Run*, p254.
[67] Bernd Heinrich, *Why We Run*, p251.
[68] Bernd Heinrich, *Why We Run*, p177.
[69] Bernd Heinrich, *Why We Run*, p174.
[70] Bernd Heinrich, *Why We Run*, p189.

(selected) the best hunters as mates. Males became the best runners because females selected them to do so.[71]

As society changes, so do many of our roles and our goals. Today's females are on the cutting edge of a new anthropological development. They are entering the hunt and where their path will lead is yet unknown.

Also, you and I no longer hunt as our ancestors did. Yet the urge is still there. No longer, however, do we hunt our prey. We hunt our limits.

The Theological Aspects of Running

The understanding of "Person" in Greek philosophy that has become a part of our cultural worldview is that an individual is made up of three separate, though connected, entities – the body, the mind, and the soul. The Bible understands there to be a "oneness" – not a blending or connection – in the concept of "Person."

Greek philosophy suggests a hierarchy as well – soul over mind over body. The Bible does not suggest a hierarchy because you are at once body/mind/soul without separation or distinction. To deal with each element apart from the other (and in a sense even to use the terms) detracts from the Biblical understanding. Yet, we do categorize in order to define.

I have discussed the physiological aspects of running (body) and the psychological aspects of running (mind). I have included the anthropological aspects of running and in doing so approached the theological (soul). Ultimately, the statement "You are created to run," is a theological statement. It speaks of a Creator and a creative purpose.

God, as Creator, has a purpose in creating. God's creative purpose is to express His essential being – love. God's love – who God is – is directed toward us.[72] The Bible describes the love that God has for us as *agape*. This love is that which gives self for the other. God desires and seeks to love us with his whole being. In a sense, God, who is love, wants to love you and me. Our purpose in being created is to be loved by God. This *agape* becomes personal to us in Jesus Christ, who is God with us,[73] God risking and sacrificing all for us, God emptying himself on our behalf.[74]

Love, however, to be complete, must be returned. We may choose to return God's love, or not. That is part of the risk God takes. The response God seeks from us is that we choose to enter into a personal, intimate, and loving relationship with Him.[75]

---

[71] Bernd Heinrich, *Why We Run*, pp 179ff.

[72] 1 John 4.16.

[73] Matthew 1.23.

[74] Philippians 2.6-11.

[75] 1 John 4.19.

The result of this loving relationship with God is life as God intended for us – life for which we were created. The Biblical word that best captures this life is *shalom*. This Hebrew word, most often translated as "peace," means so much more than a lack of conflict. It means fullness, wholeness, health, abundance, and a life integrated (fitting) with God, others, self, and Creation. It is not "The Good Life." It is the best life – life for which God created us.

As I discussed the physiological, psychological, and anthropological aspects of running, there came through, I hope, a belief that you and I were meant to run. We find evidence for this in how our bodies and minds respond to running and in our desire to reenact the hunt. I would suggest, then, that in our running we participate in *shalom* from God and experience the *agape* of God. As we read in the Book of Proverbs: "A heart at peace, gives life to the body."[76]

You can in your running find a paradigm for understanding your life within God's Creation. To run is to live in God's *shalom*. In your running you can respond to God's *agape* with joy and praise.

So why does it hurt to run? I do not know.

I do know we live in a fallen Creation that has been torn from God's intention. I also know that in all things God works for his purpose for me.[77] I know that in suffering I am measured, I am defined, I am stripped of all pride and pretense, and I know God. In suffering I most significantly encounter the God who loves me in Christ and suffers for me. I know that in suffering either I am beaten or I am thrown back on God and not myself. I discover that I can do everything through Him who strengthens me.[78]

I do not run because I am the best. I do not run to dominate you. I run because it gives God pleasure.[79] I run to proclaim the power of God's love for you.

"Whatever you do, work at it with all your heart, as working for the Lord, not for men."[80]

-Paul

---

[76] Proverbs 14.30

[77] Romans 8.28.

[78] Philippians 4.13

[79] Eric Liddell, in *Chariots of Fire*.

[80] Colossians 3.23.

2 MY SPORTS HEROES AND MODEL ATHLETES

I have two sports heroes. They are persons who excel in sports, but whose lives are more than athletics. They both are followers of Jesus Christ.

Eric Liddell

Born in China, in 1902, the son of Scottish Protestant missionaries, Eric Liddell enrolled in the University of Edinburgh where he studied for the ministry and was an outstanding rugby player – playing for his college and for Scotland. Known as "The Flying Scotsman," Liddell was never beaten in the 100m dash, but refused to compete in the 100m in the 1924 Olympics, because it would require him to run on Sunday. Many of his countrymen accused him of being a traitor and disloyal to his king. Switching events, Liddell won gold in the 400m (and set a world record) and bronze in the 200m.

Liddell's unorthodox running style – head thrown back and arms flailing – drew many comments. Both his story and his running style are captured in the movie, *Chariots of Fire*.

After the Olympics, Eric returned to China to serve his Lord. When the Japanese invaded China in 1941 he would not leave, preferring to stay with his congregation. He died in a Japanese prison camp just months before the end of the war. He was 43. During his 400m race in the Olympics he carried a scribbled note that read: "He who honors God, God will honor him."

Billy Mills

Orphaned at age 12 and growing up in poverty, Billy Mills turned to running – a tradition among his people, the Ogala Sioux – to escape the disappointments of his life. He was given a scholarship for Cross Country and Track at the University of Kansas. After an inconsistent and disappointing college career, Mills quit running during his senior track season. His coach was constantly telling him he had no heart and no finishing kick.

Mills left college and entered the Marine Corps, receiving a commission as a Second Lieutenant. He trained on his own while in the Marines and qualified for the 1964 US Olympic team in the 10,000m and the Marathon. His best time in the 10,000m was almost a full minute slower than that of the favorite, Ron Clarke of Australia.

The pre-race media coverage of the 10,000m focused on Clarke and his expected duel with Mohammad Gammoudi of Tunisia. Mills was the unknown runner. After setting the pace through the first twenty-four laps of the 10,000 meters, in the last (25th) lap Mills found himself bumped off stride, pushed to the outside lane, passed, and boxed in by the expected front runners. Mills, however, found an untapped source of strength and kicked his way to Olympic Gold, setting an Olympic record, and lowering his personal best by forty-six seconds. Mills is the only American ever to win the Olympic 10,000m. Mills also ran the marathon in the 1964 Olympics – the most grueling endurance double possible.

Billy Mills is a follower of Jesus Christ and works through several organizations for the betterment of Native Americans. His story is told in the movie, "Running Brave." The following is a transcript of the television commentary of Mill's last lap:

Voice 1: And here we go in the final lap for the Gold Medal in the 10,000m. And out front is Bill Mills pressing Ron Clarke the world champion. Bill Mills, of the United States, number 722, is leading Ron Clarke. And in third place right now is Mohammad Gammoudi of Tunis, a tremendous upset if Bill Mills can hang on.

[At this point Mills is shoved into lane three by Clarke, as Clarke squeezed between a lapped runner and Mills. While Mills is recovering his balance in lane three Gammoudi passes him as well as Clarke.]

Voice 1: But Gammoudi goes out ahead. Its Gammoudi right now leading in the 10,000m run. Clarke is third. Rather, Bill Mills is in third, Ron Clarke is in second right now. This is the final lap of the 10,000m. Mohammad Gammoudi of Tunis is putting on a tremendous sprint. He's out ahead of Ron Clarke. Bill Mills of the United States is in third. This will certainly be the fastest 10,000m ever run by an American.

[At this point Mills coming out of the final turn is boxed in by five runners who are being lapped. He is about 15m behind Gammoudi and Clarke and in lane five.]

Voice 1: Here they come down the final [inaudible]. Can Ron Clarke catch Gammoudi? They're going through the field. He's coming up. He's passing Gammoudi.

Voice 2: Look at M….

Voice 1: Clarke has passed….
Voice 2: LOOK AT MILLS! LOOK AT MILLS!
Voice 1: MILLS IS COMING ON! MILLS IS COMING ON!
Voice 2: WHOOHOOHOOHOO!
Voice 1: IT MIGHT BE BILL MILLS. WHAT A TREMENDOUS SURPRISE THIS….
Voice 2: AHAHAH!
Voice 1: BILL MILLS…THE UNITED STATES….WINS THE 10,000M!!

The following is a remembrance from one who watched Mill's race on television as a teenager:

I knew he was gonna win when I saw him. I could just feel it, like a thunderstorm coming in August. Even on the other side of the world, I could tell. He's a United States Marine.

It's our new color set, and everybody looks kind of orange, but I can tell they're moving fast. The guy announcing from Tokyo says 10,000 meters is a little over 6 miles! I can't run two blocks in gym class. I ask Dad and Grandpa how anybody can run for 6 miles, let alone so fast, and they don't know either. Dad's a football fan, and Grandpa's a baseball nut, and they only know about sprinting.

The TV guy keeps saying it's very surprising to see Billy Mills doing so well, right up there lap after lap with the Australian guy who has a crew cut as short as Billy's and as much muscle in his shoulders, too. There's a little tiny guy from Tunisia right behind these two big guys, but everybody else that everybody thought would do great before the race is pretty much out of it. The guy who won it last time is way back, and so is the guy who won the 3 miler the same year. That guy Lindgren, who's only three years older than I am and who beat the Commies in this same sort of race this summer's got a sprained ankle and he's out of it too.

The Australian guy's name is Clarke; the announcer just said it, and I'll remember it 'cause he looks like Clark Kent half-changed in Superman. He looks like he eats barbed wire for lunch. He keeps trying to run away from our guy, but Billy always catches up with him. Even I know why, from junior varsity wrestling: Billy's got nothing to lose. Clarke has everything to lose.

It's the last lap and Dad's put down his drink and Grandpa's drink's getting warm and these guys are running faster than before. Billy and Clarke are shoulder-to-shoulder just ahead of the little Tunisian guy whose name's Mohammed Something and now I'll remember it because that's the name of his god or something. It just got like football, and Dad's shouting! Mohammed just put his arms between Billy and Clarke and shoved 'em both aside! They both almost fell. Geez, they oughta slug that little geek! They're both really mad, and Clarke's right on Mohammed's heels but Billy's about 3 yards back and there's only a turn and a straightaway to go.

HE'S GONNA DO IT! I KNEW IT! Lookit him go... Dad's screamin' like it was Jimmy Brown about to score for Syracuse. HE GOT HIM! There's the little thread, he's gonna do it, he's got his hands up in the air and a big smile on his face and he's got leg muscles the size our Buick and the announcer says it's a new Olympic record and no American's ever done anything like this before.

They're interviewing him now and his father was a Sioux Indian and he is a Marine Lieutenant and he has an Olympic gold medal for running 6 miles.

You can't get any more American than that.[81]

"God has given me the ability. The rest is up to me. Believe. Believe. Believe."[82]

-Billy Mills

"Your life is a gift from the Creator. Your gift back to the Creator is what you do with your life."[83]

-Billy Mills

The Greatest Athletes I Know

I have had the honor of knowing two great athletes. I was their coach. I am their father. They are my daughter Heather and my son William.

Heather earned sixteen varsity letters in four sports in her high school career at Kentucky Country Day. She was team captain her senior year in all four sports – field hockey, basketball, softball, and track. She had five state championship appearances in three sports. Her name appears in the gymnasium of her high school four times for her leadership and abilities.

Heather earned an academic scholarship and an athletic scholarship at the University of Louisville for field hockey. She began her freshman year on the bench and did non play until half-way into the season, when she became a starter.

In her sophomore year, there was a new coach, and again she began the season on the bench. Again she captured a spot in the starting lineup half way through the season. She would never give it away.

Her junior year she was elected captain and made the all-conference team. In her senior year, she was again captain and helped lead her team to a school record number of victories and a first ever national ranking.

The first home game of her senior year defined who she was. She was the second rusher on a corner shot, and a high shot caught her in the mouth, fracturing ten teeth and requiring ten root canals, a realignment of her jaw,

---

[81] Raymond Krise and Bill Squires, *Fast Tracks - The History of Distance Running.*

[82] Bernd Heinrich, *Why We Run*, p237.

[83] Bernd Heinrich, *Why We Run*, p237.

and a second round with the orthodontist and braces. She took one day off, and was back practicing the next day.

Once at a field hockey tournament, her Cardinal team was playing the second game. The coach announced to the team that there would be no national anthem since they were the second game. Heather must have had a shocked look on her face, because the coach looked at her and said, "What is the matter?"

"Coach," she replied, "I always say my prayer during the national anthem." Hearing that, the coach gathered everyone around, and sang the national anthem for Heather while she prayed.

Our son William is the most tenacious athlete I have known. His commitment and hard work earned him twelve varsity letters and sixteen school records in three sports – cross country, swimming, and track.

For four years William was the heart and backbone of the teams I coached at Brown. His leadership was evident in competitions and practices. He had a significant impact in the development of the many younger runners whom he led by example and encouragement. He is a student of sports, and coached the Middle School cross country and track teams for his senior season. The best and most successful teams I have coached have been teams where William was the leader – the 2004 cross country team and the 2004/5 swimming team.

William really shows his character in his finishing kick. Those who know him always watch for him to come thundering into the finish of a cross country race. I cannot recall anyone beating him in the last 200m of a cross country race. He translated this mental and physical strength in track by running negative splits in races.

His best high school performances in track were in the 2005 Fellowship of Christian Athletes meet held at the University of the Cumberlands. He won his heats in the 110m high hurdles and the 300m intermediate hurdles and exploded the competition in the anchor leg of the 4x400m relay.

William received academic and merit scholarships as well as scholarships for Swimming and Cross country at the University of the Cumberlands. In spite of having mononucleosis during his freshman swimming season and sitting out half the season, he came within twenty seconds of qualifying for nationals in the 500 yard freestyle. He swam one season, interrupted his athletic career to get married to Tina, and finished his college career with two Cross Country seasons.

3 COACHING IS RELATIONAL

Coaching involves developing a relationship between the coach and the runner. The relationship involves trust, commitment, friendship, and honesty. Both runner and coach need these characteristics in a healthy and positive relationship. It is also helpful if healthy relationships develop within the team between runners.

Coaching Cross Country is a lot like being a dad. The coach provides the structure, preparation, and principles through the training process. When the race begins, however, the coach simply becomes a cheerleader. The runner must take everything learned and apply it to the race.

My Motivation

I was always straightforward about my initial motivation for coaching at the Brown School – to provide the athletic opportunities that William wanted. As I came to know the young people at Brown I expanded my initial motivation to provide opportunities for all Brown School students who wanted the opportunity. All the sports I coach had potential value for all the students at Brown.

I would also say that I enjoyed coaching. The enjoyment came from remaining connected to and involved with athletics. I enjoyed developing teams – molding individuals into a team. I enjoyed watching young people grow in life and in a sport.

Ultimately, the underlying motivation for all I do in life is to introduce others to Jesus Christ in positive ways. I pray that in all I did with my teams I was a worthy and effective witness to God's love in Christ and that each person – athletes and family members – only saw Jesus, not me.

My Model – Philippians 2.5-8

I would hope no one would be surprised that my model for coaching is my Lord Jesus Christ whose activity is described by Paul in his writings by using a hymn of the early church:

Your attitude should be the same as that of Christ Jesus:

Who, being in very nature God,
Did not consider equality with God something to be grasped,
But made himself nothing,
Taking the very nature of a servant,
Being made in human likeness.
And being found in appearance as a man,
He humbled himself
And became obedient to death –
Even death on a cross![84]

Those persons familiar with this passage, will know that I stopped at about the midpoint. I do so on purpose, for these specific verses may be seen as the description of what it means to be a leader and a coach.

I have used Jesus Christ as my model for true leadership throughout my life. When I was required to write an essay on leadership when I was a major attending the United States Marine Corps Command and Staff College, I used this very text as the basis for my understanding of the concept of leadership.

Leadership, as modeled by Jesus, is performed as a servant. A true leader (and coach) insists on nothing except the opportunity to serve. A coach who will lead young people will not grasp at status or power, nor will the coach insist on respect for his or her knowledge or past accomplishments. True coaching will be expressed through humility, service, and even sacrifice of self (personal and professional goals) for the sake of the runners. This model is what I use to test myself as a coach.

The Coaches' Creed.

Based on the Coach's Creed of the Fellowship of Christian Athletes, I have developed a creed for myself as a coach.[85]

- I shall pray as though nothing of eternal value is going to happen in my athletes' lives unless God does it.

---

[84] Philippians 2.5-8.
[85] Based on the Fellowship of Christian Athletes Coaches' Creed. *STV*, Jan/Feb 2005, insert.

- I shall prepare each practice and competition as giving my utmost for His highest.
- I shall seek not to be served by my athletes for personal gain, but seek to serve them as Christ serves them.
- I shall be satisfied not with producing a good record, but with producing good persons.
- I shall attend to my private and public walk with God, knowing that the athletes will never rise to a standard higher than that lived by the coach.
- I shall exalt Christ in my coaching, trusting that the Lord will then draw athletes to Himself.
- I shall desire to read God's Word, personal obedience to God's will, spiritual gifts to use for others, and the opportunity to make a difference in the lives of athletes.
- I shall depend solely on God for transformation – one athlete at a time.
- I shall live the message of God's love in Jesus Christ in a Christ-like manner before my athletes.
- I shall recognize that is it impossible to bring glory to both myself and Christ in my life.
- I shall allow God to shape my athletes through my coaching in His way.
- I shall coach with humble gratitude as one privileged to represent Christ before my athletes.
- I shall value the spiritual, physical, emotional, relational, and mental health and academic success of my athletes over winning.
- I shall treat the athletes of other coaches as I would my own.
- I shall have the same attitude toward others as Christ, who ...made Himself nothing, taking the very nature of a servant, ...and being found in appearance as a man, He humbled Himself....

4 2004 - A SPECIAL SEASON

I believed that Brown School Cross Country would be different in 2004 than in the previous years I had coached. During the previous four seasons (three under my direction), the teams had been dominated by a very special runner, Robert Halsell, who graduated in May 2004. The 2004 team would not be able to depend on Rob, but I believed the boys had the potential of being a solid varsity team. I also believed the girls could very well make state as a team in 2004. The 2004 season marked my fourth year of coaching Cross Country, and all of the runners were "mine" – they had begun their running careers with me as their coach.

In addition, in 2004 our son, William was a senior. I considered that this season could very well be his last Cross Country season. I looked forward to a special season.

Cross Country as a Unique Sport

Cross Country has some unique qualities that make it an enjoyable sport. These qualities also suggest that it is a good fit for the Brown School.

Coaching Aspects. Like most sports, Cross Country requires a lot of preparation from the coach. Analyzing runners, organizing practices within a season plan, and developing a schedule are just examples of the preparation required for every season. The sport requires a lot of thought.

Unlike many other sports, once the competition begins there is little a coach can change. You cannot call time out and draw a play. The coach becomes a manager, fan, and statistician during the competition.

Even more than Track and Swimming, in Cross Country the coach surrenders all control to the team once the competition begins. With every competition I did this symbolically with the last run out before runners were called to the line. I stood back. The team sprinted out, and the team leaders

(William and others) huddled everyone together for a last word. It became their team, not mine.

Team and Individual Aspects. Cross Country is both an individual and team sport. The team benefits from the performance of each individual. Both individuals and teams receive honors and awards. Brown School Cross Country had good individual runners in the past, but I believed that 2004 would be the year we would discover running as a team.

Most Cross Country races have finishing results that look like a bell curve. For example, first through tenth places are usually spread apart; eleventh through fortieth are packed closely together; and forty-first through fiftieth places are spread apart. An improvement of thirty seconds at either end of the bell will make very little difference for the team. The same improvement by runners in the pack can have a significant impact on the team score.

The 2004 boys' team did not have a dominant runner. We looked to our lead pack of three key runners – William Slider, Tim Blunk, and Eric Jeter. William, a senior, would certainly provide the emotional leadership and an experienced and steady presence, but all three young men needed to work together for the team to excel.

The girls' team had a dominant runner in Kelly McRoberts. We counted on Kelly for a high place in almost any race. The key to the girls' success would be Maddie Dailey and Sami Siegwald. These two runners had a good chance of making state.

Mixing Male and Female Runners. Because of the ages and talent level of most our runners at Brown School; I was able to mix boys and girls in practices without any friction. I can rarely detect anything but friendly rivalry and an acceptance of each runner working just as hard as the rest. I found the mixing of boys and girls in training to have no negatives for individuals or the team.

Cross Country at the J. Graham Brown School

Cross Country, with both individual and team aspects, and with equal opportunities for boys and girls, was a great fit at Brown. The sport, more than any other, enhanced the educational experience of every student and support the mission of the school.

I found, however, that athletics in general were not supported by the students at Brown. Cross Country in particular was not a popular sport especially among the high school students. It was difficult to recruit high school athletes to run Cross Country. This situation was due to the type of school Brown is and the type of student that responds to the school. The Cross Country runners, therefore, were truly exceptional

"Unique" is the term most often used to describe the Brown School, the district's only school with elementary, middle, and high school in the same building. Approximately 600 students in Kindergarten through grade twelve attend Brown. What makes the school "one of a kind" is its less structured environment, extensive community interactions, cross-age groupings, and diverse student population. No bells or buzzers sound between classes at Brown – a quiet change made to permit flexible scheduling. On any given day, some classes work together on a lesson while others are on an excursion to observe local government. Oftentimes students work in small groups or on individual projects. This informal environment cultivates students' skills of self-discipline, responsibility, and decision-making, ultimately enabling the students to develop self-directed learning styles. It is a community school. Brown provides a community environment to support individuals' learning needs. Brown School expects every student, staff member, and parent to contribute concretely and regularly to the greater good. The Brown School also offers a unique school-to-career program. The school expect evidence of growth and change in a reasonable amount of time.[86]

Entrance into Brown School is very competitive. The graduation requirements for the school are more extensive than other JCPS schools. The high school students consistently score among the top four (Ballard, Brown, Male, Manual) in standardized tests.[87] The faculty to student ratio is slightly lower than other high schools in the JCPS. For these reasons and others, many persons not familiar with the school think it is a private, college preparatory school.

From my observation only, Brown tends to draw and select students who are academically focused and more independent. Many students at Brown, therefore, do not immediately respond to the physical sacrifice (and the sacrifice of time) required to participate in athletics. Of course, this observation is general, but the benefits and value of athletic discipline and physical exercise are not apparent to a large number of students.

Having said that, I must also say that Brown has been a very good situation for William. We had a choice as a family after William's freshman year between my career advancement and William's opportunities at Brown. We chose Brown.

The Brown School Cross Country Affiliations

Just as Brown School has a unique academic setting, it has an unusual place within private, parochial, and public schools in Jefferson County, as well as middle schools and high schools. This uniqueness of the school is reflected in the Cross Country program.

---

[86] Jefferson.k12.ky.us/Schools/High/brown.html.
[87] On the 2004 CATS test, Manual was first, Male was second, and Brown was sixth out of 352 high schools in the state.

Jefferson County Public Schools. Brown is the smallest high school in the JCPS by far. With approximately 175 students in grades nine through twelve, Brown is one-tenth the size of most other high schools and easily one-fourth the size of the second smallest high school in Jefferson County. Brown is the only JCPS school with Cross Country in Class "A". All other schools are class "AA" and "AAA."

The Brown Cross Country team still competes on an even basis with other JCPS high schools – thanks to many talented and willing middle school runners. There are approximately twenty-five public high schools in Jefferson County. A few are unable to field Cross Country teams. In 2003 Brown School girls finished fifth in the JCPS championships. The boys finished seventh.

Brown School does have situation that helps it field a varsity team. In Kentucky, runners as young as third graders are allowed to run varsity for the affiliated high school.[88] High schools in the JCPS have "feeder" middle schools, and runners at these middle schools may run for their respective high school. With middle school runners "in house," so to speak, I could easily recruit and train middle school athletes for varsity competition. Other high school coaches had to identify and recruit middle school runners whom they did not know.

This situation not only helped the Brown varsity, but it also benefited the middle school program and middle school runners. No other JCPS school had a unified program with one coach for varsity and middle school. Because I began middle school practices with the varsity practices on July 15, the middle school runners received about one and one-half months extra training. Also, the middle school runners who trained and competed with high school runners were well-prepared to compete in the JCPS middle school championships and other local races. Brown middle school runners had greater opportunities for competition and came to dominate individually public middle school Cross Country and middle distances in track. When we had the numbers to put together a middle school team, Brown was always well-represented.

Another unique aspect of Brown was the academic requirements for participation in athletics. Brown School athletes had to adhere to the highest academic standards of any school (public, parochial, and private) in Jefferson County. A student who received less than a "C" in any course was required

---

[88] This situation was beginning to be evaluated by the Kentucky High School Athletics Association as I left Brown. This evaluation is a good thing. There probably are situations where some young runners are over-trained. I limited the mileage in training for my younger runners and tried to fit all runners with appropriate levels of competition.

to attend Study Skills after school for three weeks. An "F" disqualified a student from competition.

Grades were checked weekly. Usually, Cross Country runners had few academic problems, and the academic standards were a source of pride, not an irritation.

Class A, Region 2. Brown School competed at the Class "A" level – schools that have a student body (9th – 12th grades) of 570 or less.[89] Region 2 included public and private schools from Jefferson, Hardin, Spencer, Nelson, and other counties. Eighteen teams were eligible and usually there were ten or more boys' teams and about seven girls' teams represented at regional competition.

Region 2 was been a strong Cross Country and Track region with powerhouse teams from Bardstown, Kentucky Country Day, Christian Academy, and Portland Christian. The top four teams advanced to state competition.

In 2003 the girls (all middle schoolers) finished fifth (missing fourth by two points). Kelly McRoberts, Krysta Lathon, and Maddie Dailey advanced to state as individuals. The 2003 boys team (with only two high school runners) finished eighth and Rob Halsell went to state.

North Central Kentucky Cross Country Conference. In 2003 Brown School joined the North Central Kentucky Cross Country Conference (NCKCCC). This conference was a collection of less than ten schools that agree to run each other annually. We joined the NCKCCC in order to give us another affiliation that was closer to our collective abilities. I wanted us to get used to competing for championships.

The Four Year Plan

The 2004 season was not my last year of coaching Cross Country. Neither was it the last coaching effort at The Brown School. The 2004 season, however, was the culmination of my Four Year Plan for Brown School Cross Country. The culmination of the plan in this year was a part of what made the 2004 season special.

Certainly, I began the job of coaching the team in order to give my son, William, the opportunity to do something he enjoyed. The Four Year Plan stretched from the start to the end of his high school Cross Country career.

The plan, however, was not focused on William, rather on the team. I had established several goals in the beginning to reach at the end of the 2004 season:

- Develop a competitive boys team.

---

[89] Regions and classes are re-aligned every couple of years so that the schools are divided into equal thirds.

- Develop a competitive girls team.
- Develop one boy runner for every grade 7th through 12th.
- Finish 4th as a team in the Boys Region 2 Class A Meet.
- Finish 4th as a team in the Girls Region 2 Class A Meet.

My goals were not reached completely in 2004, but I believe that we can declare victory. The boys and girls teams became competitive in the region, conference, and county meets by 2003. In 2004 the boys' team had runners in the following grades:

- 12th – one runner (William Slider)
- 11th – one runner (Josh Chervenak)
- 9th – one runner (Tim Blunk)
- 8th – four runners (Eric Jeter, David Read, Jordan Smith, Zach Torp)
- 7th – four runners (Jay Connelly, Shelby Dixon, Isaac Poole, Griffith Williams)
- 6th – one runner (Houston Ward)
- 5th – one runner (Clay McRoberts)

In 2004 the girls did not field teams for the conference or regions, but both girls who ran in the regional meet qualified for state. The boys' team finished fourth at regions and sent eight runners (including one alternate) to state. The boys also finished 6th in the conference. In the end, we were close to reaching all the goals. We lacked a sophomore boy on the team and the 2003 girls team was two points from finishing fourth. In 2003 Rob Halsell was the individual boys' champion; in 2004 Kelly McRoberts was the individual girls' champion.

The Senior Project

This season was special also because my son, William, had his first experience coaching. William's Senior Project for graduation was coaching the Middle School Cross Country Team. I have watched him over the years working with the younger runners and I knew he would do well in this official capacity.

5 PREPARATION FOR COACHING CROSS COUNTRY

A coach in any sport has a lot of preliminary work and learning to prepare for each season. On the surface, Cross Country appears to be a very simple sport, but the sport requires a great deal of groundwork prior to the first practice.

Administration

A coach must be organized and structured in his or her approach to the sport of Cross Country. Nothing can be left to the last minute.

Certifications. The Kentucky High School Athletic Association (KHSAA) requires that all high school coaches be certified through a Coaching Principles Course given by the National Federation of State High School Associations (NFHS) and the American Sport Education Program. The half-day course is followed by a test. I received my KHSAA training and certification on September 9, 1996.

In addition to the KHSAA Certification, a coach may choose to be certified by USA Track and Field (USATF) and the Amateur Athletic Union (AAU). USATF and AAU certifications have different levels, some of which require no training and others requiring extensive training. At times I have received basic certification with these bodies in order to field teams for post-season competition.

The United States Track Coaches Association (USTCA) offers a diploma in coaching. The United States Sports Academy (USSA) offers extensive coaching on-line education and awards degrees in coaching and sports administration at the bachelor's, master's, and doctoral levels.

Associations. Under certifications I have listed several associations that may be helpful to coaches – the National Federation of High School

Athletics, the USA Track and Field, the Amateur Athletic Union, the US Track Coaches Association, and the US Sports Academy. Coaches may also find the National High School Track Coaches Association to be helpful. All of these organizations may be contacted through the internet. Coaches "belong" to the Kentucky High School Athletic Association through their schools' participation in KHSAA sanctioned sports.

The most valuable association for a Cross Country coach in Kentucky is the Kentucky Track and Cross Country Coaches Association. Annual membership in the KTCCCA is $15. Though it is not required, membership allows a coach to enter teams in the state Meet of Champions (Cross Country) and the Mason-Dixon Games (Indoor Track).

The KTCCCA web site (www.KTCCCA.org) is a wealth of necessary information for coaches and followers of the sport in Kentucky. Meet results and other news are posted regularly.

Required Meetings. The KHSAA requires a rules clinic and a medical seminar for all coaches. The annual rules clinic is free and is held throughout the state. Without this clinic, a coach is not allowed to enter a team in regional competition.

A bi-annual medical seminar is also required. There is a registration fee. The two seminars I attended provided good information.

Other meetings that are not required, but helpful are the coaches' scheduling meeting before the season and KTCCCA Area 3 (Jefferson County) meeting at the end of the season. The scheduling meeting is a good chance to get information on local invitationals. All-County teams and All-State nominations are decided at the meeting at the end of the season.

Coaching Contract. Directors of Athletics initiate coaching contracts on behalf of the school principals and Jefferson County Public Schools. Any contract should be completed prior to the start of the preseason on July 15th. Not only does completing the contract process before the season address any pay issues, it also provides the coach with liability protection. A coach should not hold practices until a contract is signed.

Hy-Tek. Gone are the days when coaches can run a team from a clipboard. A computer and internet access is a must. A coach should have use of a dependable copier as well.

Kentucky high school Cross Country and Track and Field are now using a system called "Hy-Tek" to make meet entries. On the positive side, Hy-Tek gives coaches a uniform system of registration for meets and meet managers and uniform means of reporting results. Entries are made through this system by email. A coach who cannot use a computer with some degree of competence will hurt his or her team.

ListServ. A system of communication for Cross Country and Track coaches and others within Kentucky is called ListServ. Information and communications are sent through the ListServ on the internet (email). With one message a coach can contact almost all the other coaches in the state. Access to ListServ may be gained through the KTCCCA site.

Logistics

"Amateurs talk tactics. Professionals talk logistics." That is a well-known proverb in the American military that stresses the overwhelming importance of logistical considerations as a part of any activity.

Cross Country is no different. Providing for appropriate uniforms and equipment for meets, transporting runners to meets and practices, and paying for uniforms, equipment, transportation, and entry fees is a critical part of the coach's planning.

Budget and Fund Raising. A part of the attraction of the Brown School is its unique status within the Jefferson County Public School system (JCPS). This uniqueness, though, puts Brown School athletics at a funding disadvantage.

Brown School did not have the ability to generate funds as other JCPS schools. Many JCPS schools generate funds for their sports programs through ticket sales at well-attended sports events, such as football and basketball, and through activities of large booster clubs. Brown School had neither the student base, nor the income-generating events to raise significant funds through ticket sales. There was also not a large booster or parent club for each sport to easily raise funds for "extras."

JCPS does provide equal, but minimal, support to all high schools for sports. Brown School, however, is the only K-12 JCPS school and (unlike any other public school program) fields both high school and middle school teams and that doubled the entry fee costs at most meets. In addition, Brown Cross Country often competed against private schools that fund sports aggressively as a part of their recruitment of students. One can think of Brown Cross Country as a private school program with public school funding.

Most sports are not expensive, but there are some associated costs. Coaches' salaries are covered by JCPS contract and did not come from Brown School funds. Every sport has uniform and equipment requirements mandated by the NFHS and the KHSAA that are designed for safety, sportsmanship, and fairness.

Entry fees for invitationals comprised a big part of the Cross Country expense. The Cross Country team did not need to pay officials as other fall sports at Brown School do (Volleyball and Soccer), but unlike the other fall sports, most of the competitions and invitationals in which Brown Cross Country participated were fund-raisers for other programs. The average cost per event for entering all runners at appropriate levels was about $100. The season total was about $1,000. The team depended on the school, the athletic staff, the Brown School Bear Runners Booster Club, and individual families.

The Brown School Bear Runners Booster Club. During the 2003 Cross Country season, parents formed the Brown School Bear Runners Booster Club (BSBR). Sallie Read served as the treasurer. Money was kept in an account that was separate from school funds. Informal meetings of parents at practices and meets determined how funds were used. Cross Country and Track were considered as one continuing sport, so funding from the BSBR supports both. The Swimming team that I coached purchased uniform items through the BSBR at cost.

Fund Raisers. Income for the BSBR in the 2003-4 school year came from bi-weekly bake sales and a spaghetti dinner. Each bake sale generated about $50. The spaghetti dinner raised about $350. Both activities depended on family donations and participation. For the 2004-5 year the team continued the bake sales and held a Bowlathon.

The Bowlathon cost each bowler $6 to participate. The cost paid for shoes and three games. It was held at Ten Pins Lane on Saturday, August 21, 2004. Pledged amounts toward the number of pins in three games were collected. The event was a lot of fun and the team raised about $750.

Uniforms and Equipment. The NFHS has specific individual uniform and equipment rules for runners enforced by KHSAA officials. I cover these rules and others in the team policies.

Individual uniforms and equipment are the responsibility of the runner. The BSBR provides a competition singlet and shorts at no cost to the runner. The BSBR also supplements the purchase of a warm-up suit. All other equipment items are the option of the runner. Here is a list of the uniform items and their costs to runners:

Item	*Item Cost*	*Runner's Cost*	*Paid by Booster*
White Singlet[90]	$15.00	-0-	$15.00
Navy Running Shorts	$10.00	-0-	$10.00
Navy/Gold/White Warm Up	$50.00	$30.00	$50.00
Navy Cotton Hoody	$25.00	$25.00	-0-
Navy Cotton Long Sleeve	$15.00	$15.00	-0-

I used two suppliers for uniform items. Louisville Sporting Goods and Louisville Direct Stitching provided great service. Getting orders and payments together was a difficult process. Sallie Read helped a great deal.

Transportation. Families provided all needed transportation except on the days when we worked out at the Central High School track. On those days, the team boarded a TARC bus for the fifteen-minute trip under the supervision of the older runners. I drove my truck behind the bus and carry water, equipment, and runners' personal items.

---

[90] Singlet and Shorts are required.

I was not completely pleased with either of these modes of transportation. I always had a concern about my liability and that of the schools when I scheduled a practice or competition, and runners and families had to find their own way. It was also difficult to get the entire team at the appropriate place and on time. I was also concerned for the lack of supervision of younger runners on the TARC bus, but my older runners were very mature and kept an eye on the younger ones.

Communication

An essential part of coaching is communicating. A coach must communicate with runners, parents, faculty, administrators, and other coaches and officials. My focus in this section is to review my methods of communicating within the Brown School. Since I did not work at the school, communication with runners, teachers, and the school leadership was difficult. My son, William, was a very important communication link for the team. William was very helpful in keeping the team connected.

Preseason Information. William and I started handing out 2004 preseason information at the end of the 2004 Track season. We both designed suggested off season running programs. William put together a letter and running plan for the Middle School athletes. He delivered the following letter by hand, by mail, or by email:

Dear Athlete,

I am very pleased to hear of your interest in the sport of Cross Country. Don't be fooled that this is an easy sport, for the training can be hard and demanding, but we always manage to have a fun and rewarding season. The training that you will do, however hard it may seem, will give you the confidence to know that when you line up with 300 other runners at the starting line, you will have what it takes to **run with the best.**

As your new Cross Country coach, I would like for you to know a little about me. My name is William Slider and I am currently an upcoming senior at the Brown School. For my senior project I will be coaching the Middle School Cross Country Team with some assistance from my dad (Varsity Coach John Slider) as well as my mentor (Athletic Director Marcia Morton). I do, however, have much experience in the sport, for this will be my 8th season competing in Cross Country. I have trained under a variety of coaches when I was in Middle School, including world-class athletes such as David Long (2:12 Marathoner). I also competed in 5 National Cross Country Championships and have three Varsity letters from the Brown School.

Official practice will begin on July 15th at 6PM at Creason Park (we will meet at the picnic tables which are near the playground). I stress consistency and progression as being a large part of my training program and we will be practicing 5 to 6 days per week. I will inform you of our exact practice schedule at the first practice. We will probably be practicing Monday through Friday at 6PM and Saturdays at 10 or 11AM. If you cannot make the first practice on July 15th, please let me know as soon as possible, so that I can get you the information you will miss. I will follow my dad's policy on coming to practice, in that you decide when to come to practice and I will decide when to put you in a meet. Also, we will not practice if the Heat Index is over 105 at the start of practice. In the event of this occurring on the first practice, I will be there anyway at 6PM to pass out information.

I have included information on workouts that you could be doing before practice officially starts. These workouts aren't intended to be overly difficult, but to get you ready for the start of practice. I suggest that it would be good for everyone to do these workouts; however, I recognize that some may need more or less. Therefore, I urge you to **let me know how you are feeling with the workouts**, *so that I can make the necessary changes with your workouts. Also, be sure to let me know if there are any other sports or commitments you have during the summer that could impede your participation in the practices. In any event I hope you have a good summer and if you have any additional questions about this, feel free to ask.*

Sincerely,
William Slider

Phone #: _____

Email: _____

William's preseason information was much more extensive than mine – which is hard to do. He had a great letter. His attached workouts will appear with mine in the section on off season training.

First Practice Packet. William and I compiled an extensive First Practice Packet that included team roster, prospective schedule, meet availability form, uniform order form, team records, team policies, contact information, and other items. Since we were free to add runners to the roster up to the first meet, we had to keep copies of the First Practice Packet available.

Newsletter. I used newsletters to provide runners and families with upcoming meet information and results of previous meets. My newsletter for Cross Country, *The Bear Runner*,[91] was given to runners and families on Monday practices during the season. I also posted a copy of the newsletter on the Sports Board in the lobby of the school. I put copies in the mailboxes of faculty and staff members.

In a typical newsletter I included results of the previous meet. The most important information concerned any upcoming meets – runners entered, race times, reporting times, and directions. I also reported on best times in other schools and regional qualifications.

---

[91] As titles for newsletters I used a play-on-words based on the school mascot – the Bear. The High School Cross Country newsletter was *The Bear Runner*. William used *Bear Crossings* for the Middle School newsletter. Other titles were *The Bear Swimmer* (Swimming), *The Bear Tracker* (Track), and *Bear Witness!* (Fellowship of Christian Athletes).

William, as the Middle School coach, took over the newsletter responsibilities for his middle school teams. He elected to provide newsletters during the preseason. The name of his newsletter was *The Bear Crossing*.

Email. William and I both used email to send newsletters, give immediate results, and send any quick changes or reminders to families. Though this method is efficient, not everyone on the team could receive email, so we always made hard copies of what we sent.

During the 2005 season an issue developed over my use of my own email address to communicate with parents and athletes. I signed my emails with "Yours in Christ, John. One parent objected. The Jefferson County Public School system has a policy that was interpreted to exclude my use of this signature. Because of this policy, I stopped using emails for communication. One administrator observed that I probably would not want one of my children's coaches signing emails, "Yours in Satan." My response was to ask if the Jefferson County Public Schools viewed Christianity as much of a threat to children as Satanism.

I found this policy very distasteful to me personally. It was also inconsistent with the mission and values of the Brown School. This mission was to recognize, respect, and foster the unique potential of each student in an informal environment that reflects the diversity of our community.[92] In this spirit the expressed values[93] of the school were:

1. An <u>informal and unthreatening environment of diversity</u> will create an <u>atmosphere of mutual respect</u> in which students, parents and staff will work together.
2. Each individual will be <u>encouraged and allowed to freely yet responsibly express him/herself</u>, confident that s/he will be <u>accepted</u> as capable and unique.
3. <u>Difference and diversity will act as bridges rather than barriers</u> to communication.
4. A healthy honest self-concept will promote in students a desire to learn more about self and the environment.
5. Self-discipline will be nurtured as an essential part of the learning process.
6. The adult community will maintain high expectations and respect for the achievement of each student's personal best.
7. Creativity, innovation, and flexibility will be regarded as necessary elements of education by the entire community.

---

[92] http://www.jcpsky.net/Schools/High/Brown/mission.html
[93] *Ibid.*

8. Every individual will have a responsibility to contribute back to the greater natural and social community from his/her Brown School experience.

Though I seek to live by a specific faith, I had assumed that my coaching style and personal conduct was in keeping with the mission, values, and policies[94] of the Brown School. I know I have not always in every instance reached these high standards, but I have tried. I hoped at least that my intent and spirit showed through my efforts. I did not believe my faith harmed any child under my supervision.

During the 2004 season, Marcia Morton,[95] as Director of Athletics, had the uncomfortable task of telling me that signing my emails (by automatic signature) with "Yours in Christ" was not acceptable at the Brown School. As a compromise – uncomfortable as it was for me – I changed my signature to "Yours in _____." I will say that this compromise did open some doors to witness about my relationship with God through Jesus Christ, but it never felt right. My emails to family and parishioners went out with that signature and raised some other questions.

When my coaching duties were over for the 2004/5 school year I changed the signature back to the original. It may seem trite to some, but to me and to whoever is offended by it, the signature is important. I had to find

---

[94] I cannot locate a specific written policy governing the issue in question. In the JCPS *Substitute Teacher Handbook*, p9, in the section entitled "In the Classroom" I do find the following: "[The substitute teacher is] specifically cautioned about the following: … Do not present sectarian views in religion or partisan or sectional views in politics."

The JCPS Principal's Planner pp77-8 has the following statements: "As a public school district, Jefferson County must be neutral regarding religion, but this neutrality exists in tension with the JCPS District responsibility [is] to be sensitive to the needs of individual students and their families so that no students (*sic*) are penalized because of their belief."

The Kentucky Revised Statutes provide some written guidance, but still there is no written policy regarding the particular issue in question. See the attached applicable Kentucky Revised Statutes. Frankly, these statutes do not give me specific guidance

As I understand the verbal direction I have been given by the JCPS in order to be neutral I cannot use any word that references my faith (e.g., Jesus, Christ, Lord, God, Holy Spirit) in a conversation or communication with a student/athlete or parent.

[95] I do not want to give the impression that Marcia Morton has behaved in any way other than as a friend to me. I recognized that she was in a difficult position, and I did not desire to put her in the middle of this issue.

another way to fit my faith into the Brown School's mission and values of diversity, mutual respect, and free expression.

Website and Weblog. In the past I had a team website. The runners and families seemed to appreciate it.

A web log (blog) is an excellent means for communicating with athletes and parents who could check the blog anytime they wished. I developed a blog for the teams I coached and have found them very good for communicating and storing information.[96] I was able to have religious content on the blog since it was mine and I did not require any athlete to access it.

Medical Issues and Considerations

A Cross Country Coach has to have a basic understanding of medical issues and considerations related to the sport. Coaches should have some knowledge of the typical injuries that may occur in the sport so he or she can provide advice related to prevention or treatment.

Physical Examinations. No athlete should participate in any sport without an appropriate medical examination and clearance to participate. A "physical exam" not only protects the coach, it gives assurance to the athlete's family. JCPS and Brown School policies do not allow an athlete to practice or compete without proper medical clearance. The school provides the opportunity to complete a sports physical at minimal cost.

Insurance. JCPS and Brown School policy requires all athletes to participate in the "catastrophic" insurance program. The cost of this insurance for high school students is $15. There is no cost to middle school students unless they run in high school meets.

Weather and Water. Cross Country runners in Kentucky, with their season beginning on July 15th and extending through the second week in November, can experience a full range of weather conditions. Runners must take care to dress appropriate to the weather conditions. Remember, it is easier to take something off what you are wearing, than to put something on you forgot to bring.

Heat Illnesses.[97] Distance running produces heat from the metabolic process.[98] Heat also comes from external sources – the sun and air temperature. Heat is dissipated from the body through convection and the evaporation of perspiration or other liquids on the surface of the body. Because they have a large surface area in relation to their body weight and do not produce perspiration at high levels, younger runners are more susceptible to heat injuries.

---

[96] www.kickthedustoff.blogs.com/bearsports.
[97] *Sports Medicine Handbook*, KORT, p4.
[98] Bernd Heinrich, *Why We Run*, p69.

All runners and coaches need to be aware of the possibility of heat injuries. The KHSAA forbids practice or competition when the Heat Index is above 104 degrees.

There are three different types of Heat Illness. <u>Heat cramps</u> are an extremely painful muscle spasm usually in the legs or abdomen. Cramps occur due to an imbalance between the water and electrolytes in the muscle. Heat cramps are treated by taking the person to a cool place and having him or her drink large quantities of water. Mild stretching is also helpful.

<u>Heat exhaustion</u> occurs when an athlete fails to replace fluids lost through perspiration. The symptoms of heat exhaustion are profuse perspiration, pale skin, dizziness, nausea or vomiting, headaches, rapid pulse, and possible hyperventilation. A person suffering from heat exhaustion should be taken to a cool place. Clothing should be loosened and wet cloths applied. Medical attention should be sought.

<u>Heat stroke</u> is a life-threatening emergency. A person with heat stroke may suddenly collapse and become unconscious. The person suffering from heat stroke will have flushed red skin, very little (if any) perspiration, and shallow breathing. Medical attention is needed immediately.

Heat illnesses may be avoided by wearing light weight and light colored clothing. Water and fluids should be available and taken. Eating smaller (but more) meals also helps. Young athletes may not voluntarily drink water and need to be reminded.[99]

Water. Sixty percent of the body weight of a human is water. Water is required in the blood for cooling the body. Dehydration is a loss of body fluids and results in the heart working harder to pump the blood.[100] To replace fluid losses runners should drink before, during, and after workouts. Hydration needs to take place throughout the day – not just during practices.

As a rule I brought a barrel of ice water to practices. I encouraged runners to stop as needed, and often I told them to take water.

Lightning. Another weather concern is lightning. Our rule for the team was during practices if you heard thunder or see lightning, then return to the team area if possible. If I saw lightning I was required by the KHSAA to suspend practice for thirty minutes after the last observed episode.

Most lightning strikes occur between 2:00pm and 6:00pm. June, July, and August are peak months for lightning strikes.[101]

Nutrition and Supplements. I have dealt with diet already in the section on the physiology of running. Let me reiterate that I do not recommend any supplements or additives. A multi-mineral and vitamin pill is sometimes helpful, but nothing is better than a well-balanced diet.

---

[99] Larry Greene, *Training Young Distance Runners*, p28.
[100] Larry Greene, *Training Young Distance Runners*, p28.
[101] *Sports Medicine Handbook*, KORT, p5.

Training Kit. Even a Cross Country team should have a training kit. The kit should include basic first aid supplies, athletic tape, scissors, elastic bandages, cold packs, and any other materials deemed necessary. It is also helpful to have some pliers and extra spikes.

Female Runners.[102] Coaches, parents, and female runners themselves should be aware of (not alarmed about) several issues related to the response of the female body to running. These issues are both physiological and cultural.

Poor nutrition is often found in female athletes. Poor nutrition underlies symptoms such as tiredness, performance plateaus or decreases, burnout, and repeated injuries. Female athletes may diet more aggressively than their non-athletic counterparts. They diet in order to loose weight to improve performance.

Few girls can get by with less than 1200-1500 calories per day. Extremely low fat (below 10%) diets have risks for females even if the overall caloric intake is good. The consequences of low fat diets include low energy and performance, deficiencies of iron, zinc, magnesium, and folate, as well as vitamins E, B^6, B^{12}, C, and A. These minerals and vitamins require fat in order to be absorbed by the body.

Female athletes are prone to iron deficiency. Girls require 18mg of iron per day. Most girls do not get that much, and excessive perspiration can increase iron loss. Menstruation increases the need for iron intake. Iron deficiency without anemia often occurs in young female athletes. Iron-rich foods, dietary supplements, and vitamin C which helps absorb iron are helpful. Caffeine blocks iron absorption.

Calcium is another nutrient where female athletes have a higher need than males. Most girls fall short of their calcium needs. Half of all female runners do not get enough calcium. Stress fractures can sideline a runner for an entire season and are the most tangible immediate risks of calcium deficiency. Jumping and running increase the risks created by low levels of calcium in the body.

There are three major physiological issues for females related to diet. These three issues are called the Female Athletic Triad – amenorrhea, eating disorders, and osteoporosis. These three issues are of growing concern due to the increasing pressure on adolescent girls to maintain an "ideal" body weight.

Athletes are not immune to these cultural pressures. In fact, many sports easily lend themselves to further increasing the pressure to be thin that girls feel. Distance running is a sport where girls frequently are concerned about their weight and appearance. This concern can lead to eating disorders

---

[102] "Nutrition for Female Athletes," Karen Sarpolis.

ranging from poor nutritional habits to anorexia and bulimia. Eating disorders can result in serious endocrine, skeletal, and psychiatric disorders.

Amenorrhea is the lack of menstrual periods. A larger number of female athletes have amenorrhea than the five percent (5%) of the general female population. Why athletes sometimes stop having their periods or have irregular periods is not known, but the correlation between athletes and increased occurrence of amenorrhea exists.

Decreased estrogen levels associated with amenorrhea may be the cause of premature osteoporosis found among female athletes. Osteoporosis is the loss of bone mass.

Premature osteoporosis is treated by reducing training intensity and providing nutritional counseling. Osteoporosis may also be the result of low calcium intake or absorption. Calcium requires fat in the diet in order to be absorbed. A source of calcium and adequate fat in the diet will help avoid premature osteoporosis.

Injuries. I have placed this section on injuries in the chapter about preparation for coaching because it is too late to learn about an injury when it happens. A coach needs to have a basic knowledge of potential injuries before the season begins. Runners needed to be warned of possible injuries in training from the course, the weather, or the strain of running.

Muscle Strains.[103] The coordination of muscle action in running is very complex. Injury to a muscle is often called a strain, pull, or tear. Muscle strains are prevented by proper warm up.

There are three levels of muscle strains. A first degree strain is a minimal stretching of the muscle-tendon unit without permanent injury. The runner will complain of mild soreness in the area. A strain of this degree is usually more localized than the muscle soreness that comes from the buildup of lactic acid.

A second degree strain is more severe and is the result of a partial tear in the muscle-tendon unit. There will be a decrease of strength and mobility and slight swelling and deformity.

A third degree strain is a complete tear of the muscle-tendon unit. This tear results in severe pain, temporary deformity, and temporary loss of function.

Muscle strains are treated using the PRICE principle – protection, rest, ice, compression, elevation. Ice should be applied fifteen to twenty minutes for three or four times each day until swelling stops. Compression (firm, but not tight) with an "Ace" bandage will help decrease swelling (apply these bandages by wrapping toward the heart). If there is an obvious deformity (as in a third degree strain), you should see a physician.

---

[103] *Sports Medicine Handbook*, KORT, p7.

Ankle Sprains.[104] One of the most often injured joints in the body is the ankle. Ankle injuries in Cross Country come primarily from uneven surfaces on unfamiliar courses.

Ankle sprains typically occur when the ankle "rolls." Most injuries happen to the outside (medial) ligaments of the ankle.

There are three grades of sprains. With a Grade One sprain the ligament(s) are stretched and there is mild pain with little or no swelling. A Grade Two sprain involves a 25% to 75% tear of the ligament(s), and there is moderate to severe swilling. With a Grade Three sprain there is more than a 75% tear, severe pain and swelling, and instability of the joint.

Rehabilitation needs to begin quickly with ankle sprains. Follow the PRICE (protection, rest, ice, compression, elevation) principle through the first three days.

As soon as possible, when you can put your full weight on the injured ankle, you need to work to restore mobility and strength. Heat and anti-inflammatory drugs are helpful. A good mobility exercise is to place the ankle in warm water and write the alphabet with your toes several times.

Many athletes in other sports[105] use a product called Active Ankle that locks the joint laterally. I do not believe that this product (and those like it) is good for running except in extreme circumstances. They are cumbersome and uncomfortable for distance running. In addition, I believe that Active Ankles transfers the stress from the ankle to the knee, but I have not seen any studies on the subject.

Shin Splints.[106] The term "Shin Splints" applies to pain in the front or inner side of the leg between the ankle and knee that is usually caused by prolonged running or walking. In extreme cases, simply standing will cause pain. Shin Splints usually begin as a dull aching pain in the front of the leg. If rest does not relieve the pain, then there may be other serious problems.

Shin Splints are pain associated with the Anterior Tibial Muscle or in some cases the Posterior Tibial Muscle. These muscles are encased in a thin sheath and attached to the foot. As long as the foot is properly aligned and

---

[104] *Sports Medicine Handbook*, KORT, p21.

[105] One of the sports I coached was volleyball. This coaching experience led to officiating high school volleyball. Over my officiating "career" I have noticed an increase in the use of Active Ankle braces by volleyball players. When I played volleyball I did have both ankles injured, but one of these sprains was due to returning to play too soon after the first sprain in the other ankle. I also broke a bone in my foot with this second sprain. I still am reluctant to endorse the use of this brace – especially for runners. The brace seems to me to stress other joints and bones in the leg and reduces mobility.

[106] "Shin Splints," ourfootdoctor.com. Ira Meyers, "Shin Splints in High School Runners."

the muscles are functioning correctly, there is no problem or pain. If the runner's foot over pronates or over supinates (causing the muscles to twist within the sheath) there can be tearing or rubbing of the muscles resulting in inflammation and pain. Shin Splints may be traced to any number of causes – inappropriate shoes, excessively worn shoes, rapid increase in training, unyielding running surfaces, muscular imbalance, improper running technique, or simply thinking you have Shin Splints.

If left untreated torn portions of the muscle may die due to lack of blood flow. Increased inflammation may cause swelling that in turn puts pressure on the muscle's blood vessels and nerves, causing permanent damage to parts of the muscle.

If you have shin splints you must first relieve the pain and then look to a permanent cure. If you have this condition remember RICE – Rest, Ice, Compress, Elevate. An anti-inflammatory drug and ice before and after running may help.

The best treatment is prevention. If you are prone to Shin Splints custom-made orthotics may be helpful in realigning and stabilizing the foot. Extra shock-absorption may also help.

Knee Injuries.[107] Most runners need not worry about knee injuries. However, with the unevenness of the running surfaces in Cross Country, the increased chance of injury with muscle fatigue, and the increase in girls running, it is appropriate to discuss injuries to the knee very briefly. It is my anecdotal observation that girls who have swimming in their athletic background tend to have a higher incidence of knee injuries.

There are several kinds of knee injuries. Patellofemoral pain results from the deviation of the kneecap outside the patellar groove. This pain occurs most often in females and is experienced in the knee when moving the leg from a bent to straight position. Patella Tendonitis (jumper's knee) occurs just below the kneecap when the tendon becomes inflamed with a sudden extension of the leg.

A cartilage tear occurs when rotary force is applied to the knee as it is bearing weight. A ligament tear usually happens with deceleration and a sharp change in direction. All knee injuries must be treated by a physician.

Osgood-Schlatter Disease.[108] A knee problem that is not technically an injury is Osgood-Schlatter Disease. This problem became "popular" with the Middle School boys on the team.

This disease is probably the most frequent cause of pain in children. The condition occurs most commonly in boys and girls between the ages of ten and fifteen. It is characterized by activity-related pain just below the kneecap. Often times there will be swelling and sensitivity in the area.

---

[107] *Sports Medicine Handbook*, KORT, p19.
[108] Osgood-schlatter.com

Athletes may signal the start of Osgood-Schlatter Disease by rubbing the knee area. Also, you can sometimes see a bump developing below the knee.

Initial treatment is RICE – rest, ice, compression, and elevation. Anti-inflammatory drugs also are helpful.

Lower Back Pain.[109] Almost everyone at some point will have lower back pain. A runner may experience such pain.

Initially, when the runner complains of lower back pain, the coach must determine the source of the problem. Some lower back pain may be caused by low water intake. In this case the pain will be felt in the area of the kidneys on both sides of the backbone about the hips. The pain will result from a jarring motion such as the impact of planting the foot with each stride. To treat this problem, the runner simply has to increase water intake.

An inexperienced runner may also assume that the pain of "tying up" during hard anaerobic work is a lower back issue. With experience most runners will be able to notice this problem that is treated by more anaerobic conditioning.

Lower back pain that results from musculo-skeletal problems should be analyzed by a medical professional. Flexibility through stretching, muscular strength and endurance, and proper running form (no forward lean) will help prevent lower back pain.

On rare occasions back pain in a runner may be caused by even a small difference in leg length. There was a young man from another school in our region who had this problem. The source of his back pain was not traced to a difference in leg length of less than one-quarter inch.

Nose-Bleeds.[110] The exertion of running may produce a nose-bleed. This condition often happens in runners who are taking medications or who suffer from allergies. Usually nose bleeding will stop spontaneously. To treat a nose-bleed, have the runner sit up. Apply a cold compress over the nose for up to five minutes. If it has not stopped after five minutes, gauze or cotton place in the nostril may help in blood clotting. After the bleeding stops a runner may return to the original activity. Blowing the nose should be avoided for about two hours. If the bleeding persists, the runner should see a physician.

Academic Considerations

The Brown School had the strictest academic requirements of any school of which I was aware. At the Brown School athletes were required to maintain a "C" or above in every class. Each Friday during the season teachers reported to the Director of Athletics on the academic performance

---

[109] *Sports Medicine Handbook*, KORT, p18.
[110] *Sports Medicine Handbook*, KORT, p15.

of every athlete in their classes. If an athlete fell below a "C" in any class, the athlete had to attend Study Skills for three weeks (fifteen days). Study Skills were held every day after school for one hour. Participation in Study Skills took precedence over any practices or competitions that are held at the same time. An athlete was ineligible to practice or compete after the third time assigned to study skills or when he or she had a reported "F" in a class.

6 FORMING THE TEAM

When forming a Cross Country team, the coach needs to recruit new runners, develop a commitment in new and returning runners, evaluate runners, assign leadership roles, and establish team policies. All these tasks must be accomplished prior to the start of preseason practice.

Recruiting New Runners

Cross Country was a "hard sell" at Brown and at Shawnee. I tried to understand the reluctance of students to participate in Cross Country. I am sure this reluctance has to do with the invisibility of the sport at the school, the lack of encouragement for certain athletics at the school, and the personal commitment that the sport requires.

Cross Country, however, would seem to be a natural fit for the typical student that is attracted to Brown. It is an individual sport within a team context. At Shawnee it could have been a good companion sport for the ROTC program and a preparation for Basketball.

I tried to identify potential runners throughout the school year. I observed students. I received referrals from teachers and runners. William was helpful at Brown in recruiting runners. Any referrals or suggestions were aggressively pursued.

Toward the end of the school year I posted a sign up sheet for the coming season. I also contact runners from the previous year.

I have not been given much support in contacting new students. I try to attend new student orientations.

Shawnee High School also had an English as Second Language program located in its building. Though these students counted toward the classification of the school for sports, they were athletically ineligible. I often wondered about the kind of team I could have as I watched the Kenyan ESL students boarding the bus to go home.

The sign up sheet usually nets a large number of potential team members. When they discover, however, when practice starts and begin to dwell on the demands of the sport several students will drop from the team. When William coached, he had eighteen middle school runners express an interest in running. Only thirteen (72%) remained with the team.

In 2004 I had eleven high school runners express an interest. Eight (73%) dropped from the team before the season started, leaving the team with three high school runners prior to the start of the preseason practice.

Team Roster

The Cross Country team roster fluctuates through the preseason. Runners quit when the demands of the sport are realized. Others join late. The roster is closed on the practice before the first meet. As an example, here is the 2004 Brown School Cross Country Roster:

Runner	Grade	Sex	Experience	Varsity Letters
Maddie Dailey	8th	Female	1	1
Kelly McRoberts	8th	Female	1	1
Sami Siegwald	7th	Female	1	1
William Slider	12th	Male	3	3
Josh Chervenak	11th	Male	2	2
Tim Blunk	9th	Male	2	2
Eric Jeter	8th	Male	3	3
David Read	8th	Male	2	2
Jordan Smith	8th	Male	1	1
Zach Torp	8th	Male	1	1
Jay Connelly	7th	Male	0	0
Shelby Dixon	7th	Male	1	0
Isaac Poole	7th	Male	2	0
Griffith Williams	7th	Male	2	0
Houston Ward	6th	Male	0	0
Clay McRoberts	5th	Male	1	0

Individual Preseason Evaluations

At the end of every preseason I evaluated each runner and their potential contributions to the team. With so many young runners I knew there would be some surprises. Most of the runners, however, I knew and a projection as to their individual progress and team contribution. As an example, here are my evaluations for the 2004 season:

Graduate. During my time as the Head Coach of the Brown School Cross Country teams we have had only one runner graduate – Robert Halsell,

III, whom I had the honor of coaching for three years in Cross Country and Track. Rob is currently enrolled at Eastern Kentucky University where he now runs.

Rob is a special young man with a supportive and loving family. His father and mother, Robert, II, and Sherry, have become friends with me and Lillian. Rob and our son are good friends as well. They are a loving family who exhibit their faith in Jesus Christ.

One of the reasons William elected to attend the Brown School was that he came to know Rob through their participation together in a post season Cross Country club. Our long bus ride to the 2000 AAU Nationals in Joplin, Missouri, gave William an opportunity to talk with Rob (Rob and Will sat together and Rob's dad and I sat together).

Rob has set the standard for Cross Country runners at the Brown School. He holds every varsity individual school record in the sport. In addition, he holds the school Track records for the 400m (outdoor), 800m (indoor and outdoor), 1500m (indoor), 1600m (outdoor), 3000m (indoor), and 3200m (outdoor). He also participated in school record relays – 4x100m, 4x200m, 4x400m, 4x800m, and 3x3K (Cross Country). Rob has made the Cross Country state championship meet every year of high school. In 2003 he received the Class A Sportsmanship Award. He was Region 2 Class "A" individual champion in 2003. He also made the Track state championship in his sophomore, junior, and senior years. He was All-State in Cross Country three times, and in Track once.

The 2004 team will miss what Rob gave to the team. The team as a whole will need to replace what Rob contributed.

William Slider. (12) As the only senior and most experienced runner on the team, William entered the season as the top runner after having been second on the team for the last three seasons. William is a dedicated trainer and student of the sport. William has been named an All-American for Cross Country, Swimming, and Track by Athletes of Good News. He is the team captain and Middle School coach.

Preseason Projection: William should provide the team consistent leadership, times, and places. I look for him to set the pace for the team's lead pack in races. We need him running around 19:30 for the 5K. He has a good shot at making state.

Josh Chervenak. (11) Josh is in line to be team captain next year. Though he possesses a great deal of potential, he has had some frustrations in past seasons. In his freshman year he had a season ending injury in his first meet. Josh started his sophomore year strong, but his training and times slackened and he fell to eighth on the depth chart. At the end of the 2004 preseason Josh was second in miles run.

Preseason Projection: The team needs Josh to reach his potential. I believe Josh can run in the low 20 minutes for the 5K and be a part of the final seven runners for the regional meet.

Tim Blunk. (9) Tim is the third high school runner on the team as a freshman. Tim had a breakthrough year in 2003/4 beginning with the last half of Cross Country season and through track season. He is a quite runner who is just now learning how good he is. With a pacer he should be able to continue his improvement.

Preseason Projection: I look for Tim to join William in a team leading pack with times in the mid-nineteen minutes for the 5K. With Tim in the lead pack our team may post a good finish in the regional meet.

Eric Jeter. (8) Eric will eventually develop into a dominating high school middle distance runner. As an eighth grader he already was on everyone's list to be the top 800 and 1600 runner in Middle School track in the county. He was the only runner on the team coming into this season to have beaten William in a 5K race, which he did once.

Preseason Projection: I look for William, Tim, and Eric to form a solid lead pack for our team this season. Eric should be running in the mid- to low- nineteen minutes for the 5K. With a solid performance from Eric, we should place high in the regional meet.

David Read. (8) David is a part of the talented group of eighth grade runners that were the backbone of the team. In the past David has been hampered by some injuries, and a potential growth spurt this season may slow him a little.

Preseason Projection: I anticipate that David will certainly be a part of the "Varsity Ten" and that he could solidify a spot at the regional meet by running under twenty-one minutes for the 5K. We will definitely depend on David for good finishes in Middle School competitions.

Jordan Smith. (8) Jordan has much untapped potential as a runner. He has great natural ability, but seems to hold himself back. As he learns this sport, he will be able to unleash himself. He has an injury to his foot that took him out of track last year.

Preseason Projection: Jordan can very easily join the lead pack of William, Tim, and Eric and be a top five runner under twenty minutes in the 5K for us.

Zach Torp. (8) Zach completes the "fearsome foursome" of eighth grade boys distance runners. He was ranked second in the middle school 3200m in track for the county in 2004. What hurts Zach in Cross Country is that he also plays soccer in the fall.

Preseason Projection: Zach was able to post a fantastic 3200m time in Track last year with little training. If he is able to get enough mileage for the 5K, he will be in the group of seven regional runners at the end of the season. If the miles are there he could run close to twenty minutes for the 5K.

Jay Connelly. (7) This season is Jay's first with the team, but he is adapting well to Cross Country training. He appears to have some long sprint ability, which will be enhanced by Cross Country training.

Preseason Projection: Jay might be a season away from being an impact runner for the team, but he is an unknown factor. As he learns the Middle School distances (2K and 3K) he could very well compliment the solid group of developing seventh graders on the team.

Shelby Dixon. (7) Coming back after a season off, Shelby shows improved aerobic endurance. Now he needs to add to that some anaerobic endurance. He is willing to do the work, and that is what it will take for him.

Preseason Projection: Shelby should provide the emotional leadership for a balanced group of improving seventh graders. Shelby will probably do better at longer distances.

Isaac Poole. (7) Last track season Isaac began to explore his "inner distance runner." At one time he thought of himself as a short sprinter, but through gentle coaxing and some successes at the 400m and 800m distances He has come to see himself as a distance runner.

Preseason Projection: Isaac should begin to produce some good times at Middle School races and continue his successes in this area. I look for a mile time under 6:30.

Griffith Brydon-Williams. (7) As our team's philosopher-in-residence, Griffith has come this season taller and more focused on his running. He continues to take pride in winning the warm-up jogs. In preseason practices Griffith has shown an increased adaptation to running longer distances.

Preseason Projection: If Griffith can transfer the competitiveness he has shown during practice to races, he should contribute to the team's success. I look for him to be right with Isaac at the one mile mark.

Houston Ward. (6) Initially, Houston appeared uncertain as to how to respond to the demands of Cross Country training. He is new to the sport, but toward the end of preseason he showed an enjoyment of the longer free runs we have.

Preseason Projection: My hope for Houston for this season is that he learns to enjoy distance running and to appreciate the challenges of distance racing. He is so new I cannot make a projection for him. I sense that he will be a pleasant surprise to us all.

Clay McRoberts. (5) In his Fourth Grade year Clay already was competing effectively against varsity runners in Track. He has the ability to train long distances, and the talent to produce some quality times at the Middle School level. He could very well win the Sixth Grade Championship and will be a solid contributor for the Middle School team.

Preseason Projection: Based on last year's track times, Clay could dip below twenty-three minutes in the 5K. He may very well make the varsity ten for regionals – possibly even the final seven.

Madeline Dailey. (8) The talented group of eighth grade boys is complemented by an equally talented group of girls. Madeline is a returning varsity state meet qualifier. She plays also plays volleyball in the fall.

Preseason Projection: I look for Madeline to make state again this year, place high in Middle School races, and run about twenty-three minutes for the 5K. She works hard and it should pay off.

Kelly McRoberts. (8) Kelly placed third in the regional championships last year. She is truly the team leader, holding almost every girls school record for Cross Country. Kelly has a solid work ethic and enjoyment of running. She likes to compete with the boys on the team. Like Madeline, Kelly is an all-round athlete who excels at any sport she attempts.

Preseason Projection: I look for Kelly to be at the front of any race she runs. She should be a top finisher in any Middle School race and could very well win conference and regions. Kelly should flirt with the twenty minute barrier for the 5K all season. Given the right conditions she should crack that barrier.

Sami Siegwald. (7) A rapidly maturing runner, Sami has been putting in the miles and steadily improving through the preseason. She is small, but pushes herself in workouts and races.

Preseason Projection: Sami should finish high in Middle School races. I am looking for her to go under twenty-five minutes for the 5K and if she can get in the mid-twenty-fours, she could make the varsity state meet.

Team Leaders

My practice is to appoint captains based on seniority and past performance. I appointed William Slider as the team captain for the 2004

Brown School team. He is the only senior and has provided leadership to the younger runners in races, in practices, and in school.

William and I agreed to appoint Eric Jeter the Middle School boys team captain and Kelly McRoberts the Middle School girls team captain. Both are quiet leaders, but respected within the team as the top Middle School runners. Kelly will act as the girls varsity team captain as needed. William and I will appoint other captains for specific races as needed.

Team Policies

William and I set team policies based on policies developed over past seasons. The team policies for 2004 Cross Country covered many areas. Our philosophy was to not make a rule that would hurt the team or be impossible to enforce.

Team policies are an important part of forming the team. Runners and parents should know ahead of time the requirements of team membership and the expectations of the coaches.

2004 Cross Country Policies

1. Practices are voluntary. Runners and their families decide if they practice. The coaches decide whether a runner is fit and capable of competing in a meet. The coaches assume that if a runner is not at practice that he or she is progressing in training at the same pace as the team.
2. Participation in other sports is not discouraged. Athletes must understand, however, that practices and training in another sport will not prepare a person for the specific competition needs of cross country as well as following the cross country practice schedule.
3. Brown School policy does not allow an athlete to quit a sport in order to begin another sport. An athlete who is giving his or her best effort will find, however, that Brown School coaches are flexible in these situations.
4. Every athlete is expected to follow the rules for maintaining academic eligibility at the Brown School. If an athlete is required to attend study skills or is ineligible only the Director of Athletics will inform the coach. Brown School policy does not allow an athlete to avoid study skills by quitting a sport.
5. Cross Country practices will be held outdoors at Creason Park, Waterfront Park, inside the school, local high school tracks, and other designated sites depending on training needs and the weather. The school provides TARC tickets.
6. The coach will bring water and other necessary equipment to the practice sites with the exception of Waterfront Park. Athletes may bring their own water to practice and must bring their own water to competitions. Families are encouraged to help in providing cups.

7. Runners are released from practice and competition at the site. The exceptions to this rule are when practices are held on school days at a local high school track or when competitions are out of town. Runners should not leave practices or competitions without seeing the coaching first. Parents or other designated persons may collect their athlete at the site.

8. Coaches set aside large blocks of time (especially in the summer) for practices and competitions, and are at every practice. Coaches will wait a reasonable amount of time for a runner to be collected, then the coach will take the runner to wherever the coach needs to be or to the coach's home.

9. Runners should be prepared to run outside <u>every</u> day. Sweat pants, hats, and/or hooded sweatshirts are helpful as the season progresses. On non-school days practices will be cancelled due to weather conditions by the coach at the site. On school days if there is bad weather the team may practice in the school building. The coach is not allowed to hold practice if the heat index is above a certain level or until thirty minutes after the last observed lightning.

10. If school is cancelled or if JCPS schools are dismissed early, there will be no practice.

11. Runners should have appropriate shoes. Good training shoes are important. See the coaches for details.

12. Beginning with the first day of practice and ending on the day of the fall sports banquet team members shall conduct themselves - in school and out of school, in uniform and out of uniform – appropriately **at all times** in a manner that will bring credit to themselves, their families, their school, their team, and their sport. In the case of inappropriate sportsmanship or conduct the coach (in consultation with school administrators, if necessary) will decide on fitting disciplinary action.

13. Uniforms are required for all competitions. All runners will wear the uniforms in accordance with the National Federation of High Schools and the Kentucky High School Athletic Association rules.

14. There shall be **no** visible jewelry or tattoos worn by runners at competitions. Only "natural" hair color is appropriate. These National Federation rules are strictly enforced especially at varsity meets. Ask the coach about hair ties, hats, gloves, etc. Captains shall decide on the color of T-shirts (no printing) that may be worn under uniforms. "Jog bras" may be of any color.

15. At competitions all officials and coaches of other teams shall be addressed respectfully as "Sir", "Ma'am, or Coach." Before a race, as the opportunity is presented, opposing runners will be wished well. At the completion of the race while in the chute at a minimum the runners that finish immediately before (if any) and after shall be congratulated. When

a runner finishes a race he or she shall return to the finishing stretch to cheer on teammates as soon as possible. There shall be no trash talking.

7 FORMULATING THE SEASON PLAN

Without a plan the season becomes a haphazard collection of workouts with no specific purpose. In formulating the season plan the coach must evaluate key athletes and their events, put together a plan for the entire year, then divide the year into periods and sub-periods – seasons to weeks to days – so that everything fits together with purpose and focus.

Training Principles

Training must be as specific as possible to each element of the event on which the athlete is focusing.[111] An important element of an event is the estimated aerobic/anaerobic energy contribution to the running of the event. Training should reflect the needs of the focus event for aerobic/anaerobic performance. Again, aerobic running is accomplished within your capability to use oxygen. Anaerobic running is oxygen debt – running outside your capability to use oxygen. The estimated aerobic/anaerobic contribution for selected events in Track are as follows:[112]

Distance	Aerobic Contribution	Anaerobic Contribution
400m	30%	70%
800m	57%	43%
1600m	76%	24%
3200m	88%	12%
5000m/5K	93%	7%

---

[111] Peter Coe, *Winning Running*, p65.
[112] Larry Greene, *Training Young Distance Runners*, p36.

Heart rate is the best field measure for your response to training.[113] There are three heart rates of which you should be aware – Maximal Heart Rate (MHR), Training Heart Rate (THR), and Resting Heart Rate (RHR). Assuming good health, your MHR may be estimated by subtracting your age from 220.[114] The MHR for a fifteen year old is 205 beats per minute (bpm).

THR varies with the focus of the workout. For aerobic training THR = 65-75% of MHR; for anaerobic THR = 85-100% MHR; and for threshold training (where fatigue sets in) THR = 75-85% MHR. The following chart may provide some help:

Age	MHR	Anaerobic THR	Aerobic THR
12	208 bpm	175+bpm	135+bpm
13	207 bpm	175+bpm	135+bpm
14	206 bpm	175+bpm	134+bpm
15	205 bpm	174+bpm	133+bpm
16	204 bpm	173+bpm	133+bpm
17	203 bpm	172+bpm	132+bpm
18	202 bpm	171+bpm	131+bpm

Your pulse may be easily taken by placing a finger (not the thumb on the neck or wrist where blood vessels are close to the surface. For an exact time count the number of beats over one minute. For an estimate use fifteen seconds and multiply by four.

Your RHR should be monitored at home at it is fun to watch the RHR lower over time as you get into running condition. When I was in my early twenties in the Marines with nothing else to but train to run marathons, my RHR would dip below 40 bpm. Young athlete's probably will not have an RHR that low. If your RHR is more than 5 bpm above normal that may mean that you have had insufficient recovery from the previous workout.[115]

Unless there is an increase in stimulation, an organism will habituate (get into a rut) and will not adapt further.[116] Training must increase in intensity in order to improve performance through adaptation.[117]

The physiological functions that you need to train for Cross Country running are aerobic endurance (base running), anaerobic endurance (intervals, tempo runs, and fartlek), speed (short intervals and strides), and strength

---

[113] Larry Greene, *Training Young Distance Runners*, p43.

[114] Larry Greene, *Training Young Distance Runners*, p44.

[115] Larry Greene, *Training Young Distance Runners*, p44.

[116] Peter Coe, *Winning Running*, p64.

[117] Peter Coe, *Winning Running*, p66.

(hills). Though aerobic training raises the maximum steady state,[118] attention should be given to all areas.

Interval training may be very beneficial when done properly. Interval training should specify the frequency of practices, the number of set in a practice, the number of repetitions in a set, the distance to run, the target time, and the duration of the recovery. Any of these factors may be manipulated to increase intensity.[119]

Runners under the age of fifteen can handle a great deal of aerobic training because their capacity to use oxygen in relation to their body weight is greater than an adult.[120] These ages are ideal for developing the runner's aerobic base.

Runners under the age of fifteen, however, cannot tolerate much anaerobic training. At distance between 300m and 600m they stress themselves too much.[121]

Much has been made of Kenyan runners and their training secret. The Kenyan secret is no secret at all. Their training is very high in aerobic mileage; they do not do excessive anaerobic workouts; they consume no diet supplements; and they usually do not wear shoes, which allows their feet and ankles to function normally and more efficiently.[122]

Rest is an important part of training. Hard training is intense and places the athlete on the edge of physical collapse. Well-trained athletes are more prone to infections.[123]

Athletic improvement comes during adaptation. Adaptation is an organism's response to stimulation (stress).[124] Rest and recovery is essential because that is when adaptation occurs.

For Middle School runners I try to maintain five days of running including competition, and two days of rest. High School athletes and older should rest every seventh day.[125]

It is hard for younger runners to be patient. Though some success may arrive immediately, you should be prepared to invest four years before you reach your potential.[126]

[118] Arthur Lydiard, *Distance Training for Young Athletes*, p19.
[119] Peter Coe, *Winning Running*, pp64-5.
[120] Arthur Lydiard, *Distance Training for Young Athletes*, p13.
[121] Arthur Lydiard, *Distance Training for Young Athletes*, pp13-4.
[122] Arthur Lydiard, *Distance Training for Young Athletes*, p23.
[123] Peter Coe, *Winning Running*, p15.
[124] Peter Coe, *Winning Running*, p64.
[125] Peter Coe, *Winning Running*, p17.
[126] Arthur Lydiard, *Distance Training for Young Athletes*, p15.

Do not be frustrated. Be patient. Kip Keino, when he was fifteen, could only manage a 5:56 mile. He later became the first in the line of great Kenyan runners.[127]

Focus Events

The athletes who ran Cross Country at the Brown School in 2004 for the most part were Track runners who enjoy Cross Country and use it to prepare for Track. Some were involved in other sports throughout the year. A few only ran Cross Country.

Based on 2004 Track performances, I determined that there were several athletes – two girls and five boys – who could form the nucleus of the 2005 Track team. These runners would not be special "coach's favorites," but an analysis of their Track events would be the basis for developing a focus event (or focus events) around which I would build a year-long training program to peak in late May 2005.

These athletes and their projected track events for 2005 were:

- William Slider, Senior, 200m, 400m, 800m, 300m hurdles.
- Tim Blunk, Freshman, 400m, 800m.
- Madeline Dailey, 8th grader, 200, 400, 100m hurdles, 300m hurdles.
- Eric Jeter, 8th grader, 400m, 800m, 1600m.
- Kelly McRoberts, 8th grader, 400m, 800m, 1600m.
- Zach Torp, 8th grader, 3200m.
- Clay McRoberts, 5th grader, 3200m.

These seven runners and their events suggested to me two training foci for the 2004 Cross Country season – 800m and 3200m. Cross Country provided a great background for these two focus events.[128] During practices in July and August before the start of school as a distance base was developed there was little difference between the two groupings of runners. As the team moved onto the track for speed and anaerobic work once or twice a week, these groups were split for more specialized work focused on the two events.

Periodization and Single Peak

American Cross Country and Track in high schools are organized in such a way as to require athletes to reach peak performances two (or even three) times in one year – early November for Cross Country, early March for Indoor Track, and late May for Outdoor Track. I preferred to have a consistent and year-long focus for the athletes with one peak in late May or

---

[127] Bernd Heinrich, *Why We Run*, p194.
[128] Peter Coe, *Winning Running*, p62.

early June for Outdoor Track. Indeed, double or triple peaking will certainly diminish the quality of the primary peak and possibly the quality of any or all the peaks.[129] With the understanding that a single peak over an academic year better serves my runners than multiple peaks, I determined that the peak for the school year would be late May for Outdoor Track when the regional meet would take place.

Having established the peak for the year, I could then divide the year into training periods. This task is called periodization. In periodization, the entire year is divided into periods and sub-periods in order to organize progression, intensity, and consistency of workouts to increase performance toward the peak. Each workout should fit into this periodization and contribute to the peak. The periodization plan for 2004-2005 looks as follows:

- **Rest** – from after the 2004 state Track Meet to the start of preseason Cross County (June 1 through July 14). Runners were free to pursue other sports, summer track events, or a schedule of easy running that I gave them to do on their own. Some I am sure did nothing, but that was their choice.
- **Base 1 – Preseason Cross Country** – from July 15th to the first meet (September 4th). This period included four days of distance runs (three for Middle School runners), one day of hills, and one day of speed play or tempo running. I also offered water running and swimming in the mornings on Monday, Wednesday, and Friday until the beginning of school. When school started on August 17th I substitute a day of intervals on the track for the tempo run. For the top runners mileage should reach about fifty miles per week. Strides and techniques followed workouts throughout the Cross Country period.
- **Base 2 – Developmental Season Cross Country** – from the first meet to the meet prior to the conference championships (September 4th through October 15th). During this period runners got used to competition, worked on qualifications for regions, and experimented. Adjustments were made to the training schedule to allow for appropriate rest before meets. Mileage did drop gradually.
- **Base 3 – Championship Season Cross Country** – from the conference meet to the state championship (October 16th through November 13th). The regional teams were selected during this period. Mileage continued to drop gradually. Hills were no longer a part of the workout and another day of intervals was added. Rest before and recovery from competition was important. Some runners

---

[129] Peter Coe, *Winning Running*, p79.

continued by choice to run in USATF and AAU events through December 11th.

- **Transition** – from the last Cross Country meet to the beginning of Outdoor Track practice (March 1st). During this period I encouraged Swimming and/or Indoor Track, but some athletes moved into Basketball. A few did nothing. This period was a time for building anaerobic endurance, continuing the aerobic base, strengthening the upper body, and improving speed. Swimming provided a means for a runner to do the first three. Indoor track began the process of developing the runners "Track legs" and also was a time to work on hurdling or other techniques.

- **Peak 1 – Developmental Season Track** – from the first outdoor practice (March 1st) to about May 1st. The focus here was to continue to develop anaerobic endurance and each athlete's understanding of his or her events.

- **Peak 2 – Championship Season Track** – from about May 1st to the last track meet. The final touches to the runners speed and techniques were the focus here. Confidence grew for the peak – regional competition.

The Cross Country Season Plan

In 2004, once we had the athletes, the single peak focus events, and all the preparation completed, William and I turned to the task of developing the season plan. He and I worked closely together, using our combined experience to construct the best plan possible for the team.

The Building Blocks. There are five essential building blocks for a successful Cross Country season. The coach supplies three of the blocks during practices, the runner supplies two of the blocks during practices and competition.

During practices the coaches provide the following:

- Progression – There is a plan to the season and each workout progresses through the season to bring each runner to his or her highest level of performance.

- Intensity – Each workout (some more, some less) will have within it an element that will challenge the runner beyond what he or she believes can be done. Portions of some workouts are designed to extend runners beyond what they have accomplished before.

- Consistency – There is consistency within each workout and throughout the season. The overall plan assumes (but does not require) consistent attendance and effort.

During practices and in competition the runner and only the runner will and can provide the following:

- Enjoyment – A coach cannot make a sport fun. The runner must find enjoyment in the sport itself – practices and competition.
- Effort – Excellence comes before success. If a runner puts effort into excelling each moment, then success will follow.

Training Needs. I have already written about the body's response to training and the various training needs for runners in sections above. What is important here is that in constructing the season plan, William and I were aware of and focused on the need to train the runners in several ways – aerobic endurance, anaerobic endurance, strength, speed, and technique. All five of these areas not only fed into the progression, consistency, and intensity of the whole; but within themselves there also needed to be progression, consistency, and intensity. In short, every workout had and purpose and fit into the overall plan.

Weight Lifting. Brown School Cross Country did not have the facility or opportunity for training with weights.[130] I am very uncomfortable encouraging any training that I cannot supervise.

As a rule Middle School runners should not attempt any serious weight lifting – especially anything requiring lifting above the head. Bicep curls and other simple exercises with dumbbells are fine, but not required. Serious lifting can wait until age fourteen or fifteen.

William did lift two or three times per week. His upper body work was high repetition and low weight. For his legs he tries to maintain his strength for Track. I do recommend leg curls (2 sets of twenty-five) to help avoid hamstring pulls from exhaustion.

Abdominal Strength. The abdominal (stomach) muscles are a critical part of any athlete's conditioning. Abdominal muscles are particularly important for running. Training the abdominal muscles has recently been the subject of more misinformation and mythology than any other part of the human anatomy. Though I would not suggest that Middle School runners should overwork abdominal muscles, it is good to establish proper habits early.

There is nothing unique about abdominal muscles as far as training and response to training is concerned. The principles that apply to biceps and triceps apply equally to abdominals. The three critical elements of any training regime are intensity (muscular overload), progression (increased intensity

---

[130] Brown School by the 2005 Cross Country season did have a quality weight room. They did a good job. Given the location of our practices and the age of my runners, the weight room really did not help my team.

from workout to workout), and consistency (proper spacing of workouts to avoid over-training or under-training).

Most people do sit-ups or crunches as an abdominal exercise. While these exercises can satisfy the "intensity requirement," they are rarely employed to satisfy progression and consistency. Muscles will only develop in response to overload that is above normal. If a person does twenty crunches every day for a year, that person's abdominal muscles will only develop to that level of performance.

To force new development, intensity must increase. Adding a few crunches every day only increases duration; there are better way to get results.

Exercise equipment for abdominal muscles that is currently advertised does not allow for increased intensity (adding weight resistance). Some have rubber bands or similar devices to add a bit of overload, but it's a trivial amount. Adult abdominal muscles are capable of being developed to the point of doing crunches with weights of 100, 200, and even 300 pounds.

The top three exercises for improving abdominal muscles are weighted crunches, weighted incline sit-ups, weighted sit-ups. Weighted Crunches are performed by using a rope handle attachment on a machine, grasping the ends and pulling the cable until it is tight and the hands are resting at the side of the head near the ears. By contracting the abdominal muscles in a crunch the athlete lifts the shoulders off the floor and draws the weight stack up an inch or two. The athlete should choose a weight that will allow only do eight to twelve repetitions.

If there is no access to a low pulley, there is a good alternative. Use the high pulley that is normally used for lateral pull-downs on a machine. Kneel on the floor or sit in the seat directly under the rope handles that are attached to the high pulley. Lock the legs under the hold down. Pull the handles into position next to the ears, then contract the abdominal muscles into a crunch that raises the weight stack an inch or two. Again, choose a weight that will allow only do eight to twelve (8-12) repetitions.

For me the optimum abdominal exercise is the weighted incline situp. Lying on an incline bench, I do situps while holding a weight against my chest. The limitation of this exercise is that eventually it will not be possible to hold enough weight safely. I do a session of weighted incline situps three or four times a week. In each session I do 100 situps without a weight, then I add two and one-half pounds of weight every twenty-five situps. I increase the repetitions by five each session. So, by the time I reach 200 situps I have completed 100 with no weight, twenty-five with two and one-half pounds, twenty-five with five pounds, twenty-five with seven and one-half pounds, and twenty-five with ten pounds.

Weighted situps are another alternative. The athlete lies on the floor and does a sit-up or crunch while holding a barbell plate against the chest. The feet will need to be hooked under something.

Abdominal muscles may be worked daily, but an every other day schedule is appropriate as well. Set a goal number of repetitions (e.g., fifty) and starting with the base weight increase repetitions by at least five while maintaining the weight until the goal of repetitions is reached. Remember that improvement will only occur when the muscles are overloaded.

When the goal repetitions are reached with the base weight, increase the weight by five to fifteen percent and drop the number of repetitions for the initial workout at that weight. Repetitions should not return to the initial number, but to about sixty percent of the goal of repetitions.

Failure to progress (to increase the intensity of the weight or the number of repetitions) will indicate an equipment problem (e.g., too many weights to hold) or the need for recovery (rest of a day or two) between sessions. When it becomes impossible to add weights because of safety issues, lower the weight and increase the repetitions, then work toward the increased goal of repetitions.

Results can only be seen if the abdominal muscles are not covered by fat stored by the body. To remove lose fat, increase the aerobic workout (running, swimming, etc).

Remember, muscle takes up less space than fat, but muscle weighs more than fat. Therefore, a slight weight gain may be experienced when abdominal muscles become conditioned and waist size decreases.

Swimming. A good complement to running is swimming. Two of our Cross Country team also swim for the school. Swimming is a good off season and preseason exercise – especially for younger runners. Swimming teaches breathing discipline, provides good upper body conditioning, and gives the athlete a solid aerobic and/or anaerobic workout with either traditional lap swimming or water running. Swimming gives "miles" without the added stress on ankles, knees, joints, and hips. It is also good for runners recovering from injuries.

From observing William, who swam and ran competitively, I have developed a simple formula for computing swimming to running miles:

Freestyle Swimming Distance in Yards x 4 = Running Distance in Meters

Take the distance completed swimming freestyle in yards, multiply by four, and change to meters. This calculation should give an approximation of the aerobic and anaerobic effort. For example 200 yards freestyle should be the equivalent of an 800m or half-mile run.

Stretches. In 2004 William taught the stretching clinic at the beginning of the preseason. He supervised stretching prior to practices.

A consistent stretching program can save you a lot of lost training time from injuries. Along with appropriately training and choosing the right shoes, stretching is the most important activity you can do to protect your body from the rigors Cross Country. Stretching after running also reduces muscle soreness.

If not done properly, stretching can actually cause injury rather than prevent it. You should not bounce while stretching. Bouncing risks pulling or tearing the muscle. Muscles must be stretched gradually and gently. If a stretch is applied too quickly, the muscle responds with a strong contraction, increasing tension. If the stretch is applied slowly, however, this contraction reflex is avoided, muscle tension decreases, and the muscle may be stretched longer. Stretches should be of thirty to forty seconds in duration and several repetitions. You should neither push through muscle resistance, nor stretch to the point of discomfort or pain.

The following twelve stretches are recommended before and after running and in the evening:

1. Wall Pushup #1 - Stand about three feet from a wall, feet at shoulder width and flat on the ground. Put your hands on the wall with your arms straight for support. Lean your hips forward and bend your knees slightly to stretch your calves.
2. Wall Pushup #2 - From the previous position, bend forward to lower your body to waist height. Bring one foot forward with your knee slightly bent. Lift the toes of the front foot to stretch the muscle under the calf. Stretch both legs.
3. Wall Pushup #3 - Put your feet together, rocking back on your heels with your hands on the wall and your arms straight to form a jackknife with your body. This stretches your hips, shoulders, and lower back.
4. Back Scratch - Grab your elbow with the opposite hand and gently push the elbow up and across your body until your hand reaches down to "scratch" your back. Gently push on your elbow to guide your hand down your back as far as it will comfortably go, stretching your triceps and shoulders. Stretch both arms.
5. Hamstring Stretch - Lie down with one leg straight up in the air, the other bent with foot flat on the ground. Loop a towel over the arch of the lifted foot, and gently pull on the towel as you push against it with your foot. Push only to the point where your muscles contract. Stretch both legs.
6. Quadriceps Stretch - Kneel on your knees (without resting back on your heels). Lean back with your body erect and your arms to the side. Hold for 15 seconds.
7. Heel To Buttock - Stand on one foot, with one hand on a wall for balance. Hold the other foot with the opposite hand and raise the heel of the lifted foot to the buttocks (or as close as comfortably possible), stretching your quadriceps. Keep your body upright throughout. Change legs and repeat.
8. Hip & Lower Back Stretch - Sit on the ground with your legs crossed. Lift your right leg and cross it over the left, which should remain bent. Hug the right leg to your chest and twist the trunk of your body to look

over your right shoulder. Change legs and repeat (i.e. looking over your left shoulder).

9. Iliotibial Band Stretch - Lie on your side with both legs bent in running position. Bring the bottom leg toward your chest and then bring the top one back toward your buttocks, so that the running position of your legs is exaggerated as possible. Hold for 30 seconds then flip sides and repeat.

10. Hamstring & Back Stretch - Lie on your back with your knees bent. Hug your shins to your chest to stretch your hamstrings and lower back.

11. Bridge - Lie on your back and, with your feet flat on the ground, lift your hips up until your body forms a flat plane. Repeat this one ten times for 30 seconds each to stretch your quads and lower back.

12. Groin Stretch - Seated, put the soles of your feet together. With your elbows on the inside of your knees, gradually lean forward and gently press your knees toward the ground.[131]

Technique Work. We had several technique drills that we developed for Track. These techniques were designed to develop strength and proper running form. William added to these drills, taught them, and supervised them. We do them once or twice per week. Runners perform drills for about 20m, then jog 20m. When rested they repeat the same drill to return to the start.

- Groucho Walk – With the lead leg, step forward in a slow running motion planting the lead foot. Lower the trail knee to the surface. The lead heel should be just even with the point where the trail knee touches. Use exaggerated arm running motion to keep balance. Lift the body using the lead leg and repeat the process alternating legs.

- Penguin Run – With straight knees and little arm motion run from the "ankles" by pushing off on the balls of the feet. Propel the body forward by using ankle flip only.

- High Knee – Run with high knee and arm action. Keep the trunk of the body as straight as possible with no backward or forward lean.

- Fast Feet – Run with short fast strides concentrating on a light touch on the surface. Do not slam the feet down or shuffle.

- Grapevine – Run sideways crossing the legs over. Keep the torso parallel to the direction of the run.

---

[131] Josh Clark, "Stay Loose," coolrunning.com.

- Skip – With a skipping motion throw the body upward with a quick lifting motion of the lead knee and balancing arm. Land on the trail leg, take a short step to switch trail legs and repeat the process.
- Kick Yourself – Run with short strides lifting the foot toward the buttocks at the beginning of the recovery.
- Backward Run – Run backwards on the toes. Concentrate on pushing off.
- Zig-Zag – Run a given distance in a zig-zag pattern.

Learning to Race

Younger runners especially need to rehearse racing situations. Many situations may be practiced during workouts themselves. Runners may use practices to develop a sense of pace and to understand how and why to run in a pack. Surges and pace changes may also be taught during practices. Athletes quickly learn to run the shortest distance possible during workouts.

Race tactics should be discussed and rehearsed. I taught runners to run through the crest of a hill, because many runners will slow before the top of a hill.

Tight turns must also be practiced. William learned a technique for making tight turns. Lean into the turn at raise the arms above the head to change the center of gravity. A tight turn may be taken in this manner without a decrease in pace.

I also taught runners to surge beyond a runner they are passing to create separation immediately. It is also helpful not to look back when running.

The start of a race is critical. The start determines who will be playing catch up through the first part of the race. Runners should practice pushing off the lead leg and staying low out of the start. Runners should also be instructed as to the rules and etiquette of starting – commands, run outs, stacking teams, and stepping to the line.

Runners should also be prepared for the finish. I liked my runners to make visual contact with the finish line from 200m if possible. Runners should be taught to focus on the finish. I tried to convince my runners that if they are with another competitor within 100m of the finish, then they will not be out sprinted.

8 SETTING THE SEASON SCHEDULE

Once the season plan is formed, detailed schedules must be developed. These schedules should build toward the season goals.

Goals
My season goals for the 2004 team were related to the Four Year Plan that I discussed earlier. Though in my planning Cross Country season would prepare for Track season, still we built toward County, Conference, and Region Championships.

Off Season
William and I developed separate but complementary workouts for the off season for our respective teams. For the High School runners I provided for a period of rest, then light workouts beginning one month prior to the beginning of preseason.

OFF SEASON WORKOUTS FOR HIGH SCHOOL RUNNERS

Experienced runners

- Week beginning Monday, June 14th – 15-20 miles for the week. Run no more than 5 days.
- Week beginning Monday, June 21st – 18-23 miles for the week. Run no more than 5 days.
- Week beginning Monday, June 28th – 20-25 miles for the week. Run no more than 6 days.
- Week beginning Monday, July 5th – 22-27 miles for the week. Run no more than 6 days.

- Week beginning Monday, July 12th – 3 miles on Monday, 3 miles on Tuesday, off on Wednesday.

Inexperienced runners

- Week beginning Monday, June 14th – 8-10 miles for the week. Run no more than 4 days.
- Week beginning Monday, June 21st – 10-12 miles for the week. Run no more than 5 days.
- Week beginning Monday, June 28th – 12-15 miles for the week. Run no more than 6 days.
- Week beginning Monday, July 5th – 15-18 miles for the week. Run no more than 6 days.
- Week beginning Monday, June 12th – 2 miles on Monday, 2 miles on Tuesday, off on Wednesday.

William provided a more extensive plan of off season workout options for his seventh and eighth grade runners. He researched appropriate training methods before developing his plan.

Early summer training options for 7th and 8th graders

During these first few weeks of summer break before practice starts, I would not recommend hard running for anyone. However, some training would help in getting prepared for summer practice.

- If you have access to a pool with lap lanes, I strongly suggest that you take advantage of it. Swimming is one of the best cross trainers for running since it helps build the upper body and increase aerobic endurance without stressing your joints.
- Be sure to stretch well and at least twice each day.
- Be sure to drink plenty of water, especially on hot days. Drink at least one glass (16 ounces) for every 10 minutes of activity before and after your workout.

Below is a weekly schedule and be sure to keep in mind that this should not be at a hard pace, but at a steady and relaxed one. You should be barely able to comfortably carry on a conversation while you are working out. There are two options for workouts (A and B), decide to do one each day. I would suggest staying with either all "A" workouts or all "B" workouts, but you may switch back and forth if you must.

June 10th – June 30th

| Monday | Workout A: Swim | 20 to 30 minutes |

Monday   Workout A: Swim   20 to 30 minutes
               Workout B: Run 20 minutes
Tuesday   OFF
Wednesday A: Swim   20 to 30 minutes
               B: Run 30 minutes
Thursday   A: Swim   20 minutes (Slow and Easy!!!)
               B: Run 20 minutes (Slow and Easy!!!)
Friday   OFF
Saturday   A: Swim   30 to 45 minutes
               B: Run 30 minutes
Sunday   OFF

July 1st - July 14th

Monday   A: Swim   30 minutes
               B: Run 30 minutes
Tuesday   OFF
Wednesday A and B: Run   30 minutes
Thursday   A: Swim   35 minutes (Slow and Easy!!!)
               B: Run 25 minutes (Slow and Easy!!!)
Friday   OFF
Saturday   A: Swim   45 minutes
               B: Run 30 minutes
Sunday   OFF

If you have the discipline to follow this, it should help you be ready for the first official team practice on July 15th. This is probably what most of you should do, but if you think that you may need a harder or easier workout schedule please let me know.

Have a good summer, Coach Will

Preseason

The 2004 preseason began on July 15th and ended on the day before the first meet. The focus of the preseason was development of the aerobic base. The preseason workouts are included in the Workout Calendar below.

As a part of the conclusion of the preseason, I had the team run a one mile time trial on Wednesday, September 1st. Here are the results:

END OF 2004 PRESEASON TIME TRIAL – ONE MILE

Runner	Time
William Slider (B12)	5:45
Eric Jeter (B8)	6:13
Jordan Smith (B8)	6:22
Isaac Poole (B7)	6:25

David Read (B8)	6:47
Maddie Dailey (G8)	7:04
Griffith Brydon-Williams (B7)	7:22
Sami Siegwald (G7)	7:58
Jay Connelly (B7)	8:02
Shelby Dixon (B7)	8:05
Houston Ward (B6)	8:08
Kelly McRoberts (G8)	DNR
Josh Chervenak (B11)	DNR
Tim Blunk (B9)	DNR
Zach Torp (B8)	DNR
Clay McRoberts (B5)	DNR

The Preseason ended with the Team Picnic on Friday, September 3rd. We had a hard time setting the date due to some family considerations. The picnic was simply a time for relaxing and building the team attitude.

Developmental Season
The Developmental Season included all the early meets from September 4th to October 12th. These meets provided individuals the opportunity to practice racing skills and gain experience. During this season William and I began to look at runners and their performances for putting teams together for the various championships. During this period we attempted to get as many runners as possible qualified for the regional championships with four high school meets. The developmental meet and workout schedules are found below.

Championship Season
The Championship Season is the focus of the team. Some overlap does occur with the Developmental Season. The championship meet and workout schedules are found below.

Postseason
The Postseason is an opportunity for runners to continue to challenge themselves at the state and national level with the USATF and AAU meets. These events are strictly voluntary, training is less intense, and runners are essentially on their own. Last year several runners participated, but this year no one chose to do so.

Schedule of Meets
There is a progression to the schedule of meets for a season. The attempt should be to build experience and racing fitness for the regional

championships. Since our 2004 regional championships were scheduled for McNeeley Lake Park (a difficult and hilly course) I sought meets that would build toward the regional site in terms of difficulty and hills. I knew we would sacrifice good times, but I believed it was essential to have the team "toughened" for regionals.

Meets also provide an element of enjoyment and a means to evaluate the effectiveness of individual training. I tried to give the team a consistent opportunity to race.

2004 CROSS COUNTRY SCHEDULE

PRESEASON

July 15	Thurs	M/V	First Day of Practice
August 17	Tues	M/V	First Day of School
August 21	Sat	M/V	Bowlathon @ Ten Pins Lanes
September 3	Fri	M/V	Team Picnic @ Slider's House

DEVELOPMENTAL SEASON

September 4	Sat	M/V	Tiger Run @ Seneca
September 11	Sat	JV/V	Male Invitational @ Creason
September 18	Sat	M/V	Trinity/SHA Invites @ Sawyer
September 20	Mon	M	JCPS MS Region 2 @ Creason
September 23	Thu	E/M/F	Freshman Championships @ Shively
October 2	Sat	JV/V	Atherton Invite @ Atherton
October 9	Sat	V	Rocket Relays @ Sawyer

CHAMPIONSHIP SEASON

October 16	Sat	JV/V	NCKCCC @ Walton Verona
October 23	Sat	M/JV/V	DeSales Invite @ McNeeley
October 26	Tues	V	JCPS @ Creason
October 30	Sat	E/M/V	Meet of Champs @ Lexington
November 6	Sat	V	Region 2 Class A @ McNeeley
November 13	Sat	V	Class A State @ Horse Park

POSTSEASON

November 13	Sat		USATF State @ Horse Park
November 14	Sun		AAU State @ Grant County
November 20	Sat		Region 5 USATF @ Louisville
December 4	Sat		AAU Nationals @ Knoxville, TN
December 11	Sat		USATF Nationals @ Chicago, IL

The Workout Calendar

After establishing the season focus, meet schedule, and goals for the season, William and I began planning workouts. We usually planned one month at a time to give us the opportunity to evaluate what the team needed. William was more than a partner in the planning of workouts. He not only had a coach's perspective, but a runner's perspective as well. If he felt uncomfortable with a workout, then we planned something different.

Workouts as they appear below are those designed for the top runners on the team. William and worked hard to make each workout appropriate for the age and ability of each runner, yet maintain the team aspect of the workouts. If you use the workouts found below simply decrease each workout for younger and inexperienced runners as needed.

<u>July Workouts</u>

Tue 15th	6:00PM	Parent and Runner Meeting @ Creason Park
		Warm Up Clinic
		1-2 x Basic Course
		4 x Strides
Fri 16th	9:00AM	Water Running Executive Inn
	6:00PM	Warm Up Creason Park
		HS 1-2 x Basic Course
Sat 17th	9:30AM	Warm Up Seneca Park
		1-4 x Golf Course
Sun 18th		OFF **Week: 20 miles max**
Mon 19th	9:00AM	Water Running Executive Inn
	6:00PM	Warm Up Creason Park
		Technique Drills
		2-6 x Hill Course
Tue 20th	6:00PM	Warm Up Creason Park
		1-3 x Basic Course
		4 x Strides
Wed 21st	9:00AM	Water Running Executive Inn
	6:00PM	Warm Up Creason Park
		Technique Drills
		2-3 x Hard/Easy Course
Tue 22nd	6:00PM	Warm Up Creason Park
		45 Minute Free Run
		4 x Strides
Fri 23rd	9:00AM	Water Running Executive Inn
	6:00PM	Warm Up Creason Park
		HS 30 Minute Free Run

Sat 24th	9:30AM	Warm Up Seneca Park
		1-2 x Interstate Course
		(Loop Course as needed)
Sun 25th		OFF **Week: 37 miles max**

Mon 26th	9:00AM	Water Running Executive Inn
	6:00PM	Warm Up Creason Park
		Technique Drills
		3-8 x Hill Course
Tue 27th	6:00PM	Warm Up Creason Park
		50 Minute Free Run
		4 x Strides
Wed 28th	9:00AM	Water Running Executive Inn
	6:00PM	Warm Up Creason Park
		Technique Drills
		2-4 x Hard/Easy Course
Thu 29th	6:00PM	Warm Up Creason Park
		55 Minute Free Run
		4 x Strides
Fri 30th	9:00AM	Water Running Executive Inn
	6:00PM	Warm Up Creason Park
		HS 35 Minute Free Run
Sat 31st	9:30AM	Warm Up Seneca Park
		40-80 Minute Free Run

August Workouts

| Sun 1st | | OFF **Week: 44 miles max** |

Mon 2nd	9:00AM	Water Running Executive Inn
	6:00PM	Warm Up Creason Park
		Technique Drills
		4-9 x Hill Course
Tue 3rd	6:00PM	Warm Up Creason Park
		2-3 x Basic Course
		4 x Strides
Wed 4th	9:00AM	Water Running Executive Inn
	6:00PM	Warm Up Creason Park
		Technique Drills
		2-4 x Hard/Easy Course
Thu 5th	6:00PM	Warm Up Creason Park
		60 Minute Free Run

		4 x Strides
Fri 6th	9:00AM	Water Running Executive Inn
	6:00PM	Warm Up Creason Park
		HS 45 Minute Free Run
Sat 7th	9:30AM	Warm Up Seneca Park
		1-2 x Interstate Course
		(Loop Course as needed)
Sun 8th		OFF **Week: 45 miles max**
Mon 9th	9:00AM	Water Running Executive Inn
	6:00PM	Warm Up Creason Park
		Technique Drills
		4-10 x Hill Course
Tue 10th	6:00PM	Warm Up Creason Park
		80 Minute Free Run
		4 x Strides
Wed 11th	9:00AM	Water Running Executive Inn
	6:00PM	Warm Up Creason Park
		Technique Drills
		3-5 x Hard/Easy Course
Thu 12th	6:00PM	Warm Up Creason Park
		75 Minute Free Run
		4 x Strides
Fri 13th	9:00AM	Water Running Executive Inn
Sat 14th	9:30AM	Warm Up Seneca Park
		50-90 Minute Free Run
Sun 15th		OFF **Week: 40 miles max**
Mon 16th	9:00AM	Water Running Executive Inn
Tue 17th	6:00PM	Warm Up Creason Park
		75 Minute Free Run
Wed 18th	6:00PM	All-Sports Meeting School
		Parents and Runners
Thu 19th	6:00PM	Warm Up Bellarmine Track
		4x400 or 800 Continuous Relay
Fri 20th		OFF
Sat 21st	1:00PM	BOWLATHON Ten Pins Lane
Sun 22nd		OFF **Week: 15 miles max**
Mon 23rd	2:55PM	Warm Up Waterfront Park
		Technique Clinic
		Hills and Strides
Tues 24th	6:00PM	45 Minute Free Run Creason Park

Wed 25th	2:55PM	Warm Up Central Track 1600m Time Trial Easy Run
Thu 26th	6:00PM	Warm Up Creason Park 60 Minute Free Run
Fri 27th		OFF
Sat 28th	9:30AM	Look at Course Seneca Park 75 Minute Free Run
Sun 29th		OFF **Week: 27 miles max**
Mon 30th	2:55PM	Warm Up Waterfront Park Hills and Strides
Tues 31st	6:00PM	Warm Up Creason Park 60 Minute Free Run

September Workouts

Wed 1st	2:55PM	Warm Up Central Track Technique Drills 3x600 Intervals[132]
Thu 2nd	6:00PM	Warm Up Creason Park 45 Minute Team Run
Fri 3rd	6:00PM	TEAM PICNIC Slider's House
Sat 4th		TIGER RUN Seneca Park
Sun 5th		OFF **Week: 27 miles max**
Mon 6th	2:55PM	Warm Up Waterfront Park Technique Drills Hills and Strides
Tues 7th	6:00PM	Warm Up Creason Park 60 Minute Free Run
Wed 8th	2:55PM	Warm Up Central Track Technique Drills 4x400/800 Continuous Relay
Thu 9th	6:00PM	Warm Up Creason Park 45 Minute Team Run
Fri 10th		OFF
Sat 11th		MALE INVITATIONAL Creason Park
Sun 12th		OFF **Week: 30 miles max**
Mon 13th	2:55PM	Warm Up Waterfront Park

---

[132] For an easy to follow design for personalized interval workouts see J. Gerry Purdy, *Running Trax*, 1996.

		Technique Drills
		Hills and Strides
Tues 14th	6:00PM	Warm Up Creason Park
		70 Minute Free Run
Wed 15th	2:55PM	
		Warm Up Central Track
		Technique Drills
		3x800
Thu 16th	6:00PM	Warm Up Creason Park
		50 Minute Team Run
Fri 17th		OFF
Sat 18th		TRINITY/SHA INVITATIONALS @ Sawyer
Sun 19th		OFF **Week: 30 miles max**
Mon 20th	3:00PM	JCPS MS Region 2 Creason Park
		HS Hill run
		Hills and Strides
Tues 21st	6:00PM	Warm Up Creason Park
		45-80 Minute Free Run
Wed 22nd		OFF MS and Freshman
		Others 60 minute run on own
Thu 23rd	4:00PM	FRESHMAN CHAMPIONSHIP @ Shively
		Others 45 Minute Run
Fri 24th		OFF
Sat 25th	9:30AM	OFF Seneca Park
Sun 26th		OFF **Week: 25 miles max**
Mon 27th	2:55PM	Warm Up Waterfront Park
		Technique Drills
		Hills and Strides
Tues 28th	6:00PM	Warm Up Creason Park
		60 Minute Free Run
Wed 29th	2:55PM	Warm Up Central Track
		4-5 x 400 intervals
Thu 30th	6:00PM	Warm Up Creason Park
		45 Minute Team Run

October Workouts

Fri 1st		OFF
Sat 2nd		ATHERTON INVITATIONAL Atherton
Sun 3rd		OFF **Week: 30 miles max**

Mon 4th	2:55PM	Warm Up Waterfront Park
		Technique Drills
		Hills and Strides
Tues 5th	6:00PM	Warm Up Creason Park
		45-60 minute chase run (hard)
Wed 6th	2:55PM	Warm Up Central Track
		4-5 x 400 intervals
Thu 7th	6:00PM	Warm Up Creason Park
		45-60 Minute Team Run
Fri 8th		OFF
Sat 9th		ROCKET RELAYS @ Sawyer Park
Sun 10th		OFF **Week: 30 miles max**

Mon 11th	2:55PM	Warm Up Waterfront Park
		Technique Drills
		Hills and Strides
Tues 12th	6:00PM	Warm Up Creason Park
		45-60 minute chase run (hard)
Wed 13th	2:55PM	Warm Up Central Track
		4-5 x 400 intervals
Thu 14th	6:00PM	Warm Up Creason Park
		45-60 Minute Team Run
Fri 15th		OFF
Sat 16th		NCKCCC Walton Veronna
Sun 17th		OFF **Week: 30 miles max**

Mon 18th		Warm Up Waterfront Park
		Technique Drills
		Hills and Strides
Tues 19th		Warm Up Creason Park
		45-60 minute chase run (hard)
Wed 20th		Warm Up Central Track
		4-5 x 400 intervals
Thu 21st		Warm Up Creason Park
		45-60 Minute Team Run
Fri 22nd		OFF
Sat 23rd		DeSales Invitational McNeeley Lake Park
Sun 24th		OFF **Week: 30 miles max**

Mon 25th		OFF
Tues 26th		JCPS Championships Creason Park
Wed 27th		Warm Up Central Track
		4-5 x 400 intervals

Thu 28th	Warm Up Creason Park
	45-60 Minute Team Run
Fri 29th	OFF
Sat 30th	MEET OF CHAMPIONS Lexington
Sun 31st	OFF **Week: 25 miles max**

November Workouts

Mon 1st	Off
Tues 2nd	Warm Up Creason Park
	45-60 minute pack run
	4x Strides
Wed 3rd	Warm Up Creason Park
	45-60 minute team run
Thu 4th	Warm Up Creason Park
	30-45 Minute Team Run
Fri 5th	OFF
Sat 6th	CLASS A REGION 2 McNeeley Lake Park
Sun 7th	OFF **Week: 20 miles max**

Mon 8th	OFF
Tues 9th	Warm Up Creason Park
	30-45 minute chase run (hard)
Wed 10th	Warm Up Creason Park
	Easy Running, Play Time
Thu 11th	Warm Up Creason Park
	Easy Running, Play Time
Fri 12th	OFF
Sat 13th	KHSAA/USATF STATE Ky. Horse Park

9 EXECUTING THE SEASON PLAN

Planning is meaningless without execution. A plan should be followed to the point where it is effective. A plan should always welcome flexibility and creativity. Adjustments shall be required. As I learned in the Marine Corps, a battle plan is perfect until the first bullet is fired. A season plan is perfect until the first race.

Tracking the Miles

The runners enjoyed watching their mileage accrue through the 2004 season. As a motivational tool I gave T-Shirts as rewards for reaching the 100, 200, and 300 mile thresholds. The Marine Corps recruiters gave me twenty shirts that I used for the 100 mile recognition. I had nine Gatorade shirts that I used for the 200 mile mark. At 300 miles I gave shirts that I got from the Coast Guard recruiter.

I only kept track of miles that were run under my supervision. I know many runners ran on their own either to make up practices or to add to their mileage.

Some athletes played other sports and got many miles in those situations. In these situations my concerns were to insure proper training for Cross Country, and to avoid injuries through over loading.

In addition, preseason or summer mileage was much higher – but less intense – than mileage during the end of the season. For example, William Slider was averaging fifty miles per week during the summer, but toward the end of the season as we rested before and after meets and as we ran more intervals his mileage "dropped," though his effort did not.

Miles do not measure every component of a practice session. As a sprinter in college I would be asked how many miles I ran. That particular day I may have warmed up, completed some drills, run 24x200, and cooled down for a total of about five miles. The distance runners on that day may have had a twelve mile run. The mileage did not reflect the equal effort.

Still, mileage does measure equally the effort and commitment of all runners since in Cross Country the workouts are the same for everyone.

At the end of the 2004 season the runners had compiled the following mileage statistics:

MILES RUN IN PRACTICE FOR 2004

Runner	Daily Average	Weekly Average	Season Total
William Slider	5.9	35	467
Eric Jeter	3.4	21	272
Josh Chervenak[133]	3.4	21	261
Isaac Poole	3.1	18	230
Tim Blunk	2.7	16	208
Kelly McRoberts	2.6	15	204
Clay McRoberts	2.2	13	173
Shelby Dixon	2.1	13	174
Maddie Dailey	2.2	12	171
Houston Ward	2.0	12	144
David Read	1.8	11	141
Griffith Williams	1.9	11	136
Zach Torp	1.7	10	135
Sami Siegwald	1.8	11	133
Jordan Smith[134]	2.1	12	110
Jay Connelly	1.2	7	88

Performance Points

In *Running Trax*, Dr. J. Gerry Purdy[135] has developed a means of scoring performances at different distances to show comparative levels of ability and effort. His intent is to assist coaches in developing interval workouts. I used

---

[133] As a varsity runner Josh had two fewer meets than Eric Jeter.

[134] Jordan Smith was injured for the last part of the season

[135] The formula for calculating performance points is: Point Score $= C_1 \times (M - z) + C_2 \times (e^{C_3 \times (M-z)} - 1)$

- C1, C2, and C3 are constants for the distance run

- M = Mark (velocity in m/seconds

- Z = Zero offset

- E = Natural logarithm (a constant equal to approximately 2.71828183

his charts for the intended purpose, but also to score runners on their relative efforts and contributions to the team over the season. The scores for each runner are as follows:

PERFORMANCE POINTS FOR THE 2004 SEASON

Runner	Average Score	Season Total
Eric Jeter[136]	413	4548
William Slider	402	4420
Kelly McRoberts	355	4280
Tim Blunk	371	3711
Josh Chervenak	364	3672
Clay McRoberts	363	3625
David Read	323	3233
Isaac Poole	332	2988
Maddie Dailey	297	2970
Griffith Williams	296	2370
Sami Seigwald	250	2560
Zach Torp	338	2029
Houston Ward	203	1420
Shelby Dixon	232	1391
Jay Connelly	132	1383
Jordan Smith	383	1150

Regional Team Selection

It should be simple, but it never is. Selecting the runners to represent the school at the regional meet is difficult.

The female runners were easy to select, since there were only three, and all three are quality runners. Maddie Dailey, Kelly McRoberts, and Sami Siegwald were named to the regional team.

For the boys there were nine runners qualified for the regional meet. Each runner had competed in four high school level meets in order to qualify for the regional meet.

The first four runners were easy to select. William Slider, Tim Blunk, Eric Jeter, and Clay McRoberts had all proven themselves in meets and were consistently at the top of the team and improving. William had finished first for the team in every race this year except for one loss to Tim. Eric and Clay were improving race by race.

The difficulty was in choosing runners five, six, and seven for the team. Runners eight and nine would be on the team, but serve as alternates.

---

[136] Eric Jeter as a Middle School runner had two more meets to run and accumulate points that did William Slider.

Of the remaining five runners from which I could have chosen, Griffith Brydon-Williams did not have quite the quality times the other runners had. He was probably a year away. Though I felt comfortable calling on him to run if needed, he would be my ninth runner.

I believed that Josh Chervenak, Zach Torp, David Read, and Isaac Poole could all give us good races, but I could only choose three of these young men to run and one to be the team's first alternate. Each boy had strengths and weaknesses. Josh and Isaac had committed more miles in training. Isaac was more consistent, yet he had the slowest "best" time of the four. David and Zach were the most unpredictable of the four. Josh had some good races early in the season, but seemed to be slowing. Eventually, the determining factors were experience, best 5K times, and best 5K times on the course where we would run regionals. I chose Josh, David, and Zach.

I was very proud of Isaac. He was very much a part of the team. He attended practices prior to regional and state. He came to both meets. I counted him as a state qualifier.

After I had made the choice I remembered that if Jordan Smith had not been injured in midseason, my decision would have been even more difficult. Jordan probably would have been our fourth or fifth runner.

10 ENDING THE SEASON

Cross Country seasons are long campaigns. For the coach the season is not finished with the last race. Several other tasks must be completed in order to end the season. The end of one season often sets the tone for the beginning of the next.

Awards

Athletes need to be recognized for their accomplishments and sacrifices. Student-Athletes deserve to be honored.

Awards Policy. For the 2004 season William and I developed an awards policy. We felt that an established policy before the season would create no opportunity for misunderstandings.

AWARDS, RECOGNITION, AND HONORS POLICY

Mileage Awards during the Season
- One Hundred Mile Award – a T-shirt provided by the United States Marine Corps – given to runners who accumulate 100 training miles.
- Two Hundred Mile Award – a T-shirt provided by the Gatorade High School Sports Program – given to runners who accumulate 200 training miles.
- Three Hundred Mile Award – a T-shirt provided by the United States Coast Guard – given to runners who accumulate 300 training miles.
- Four Hundred Mile Award – to be determined – given to runners who accumulate 400 training miles.

<u>End of Season Competition:</u>
- Varsity regional team qualification – earned by runners who compete in a minimum of four high school races. Middle School runners are eligible.
- Varsity regional team selection – the coach may select up to ten boys and ten girls to the Brown School regional team. Selection is based on time and qualification.
- Varsity regional declared runner – the coach shall declare up to seven boys and seven girls from the athletes selected for the regional team to run in the regional championships.
- Varsity state qualification – a runner may qualify to run in the state championships either by being a member of a team that finishes in the top four of the region, or by finishing in the top seven individuals in the region.

<u>End of Season Team Awards:</u>
- Certificate of Participation – earned by all runners who complete the season in good standing with the team.
- Varsity Letter – earned by all runners who make the varsity regional team or contribute significantly to the varsity team (right now this is in certificate form, but I would like to give an actual letter to students if the BSBR funds can handle it).
- Seven boys and seven girls trophies are provided by Brown School Athletics:
    - Boy/Girl Captains
    - Boy/Girl Leadership
    - Boy/Girl Most Improved
    - Boy/Girl Warrior
    - Boy/Girl Best Newcomer
    - Boy/Girl Coaches Award
    - Boy/Girl Teammate Award (voted by team)
- Six awards (certificate and shoe bag) are provided as a part of the Gatorade High School Sports Program:
    - Player-of-the-Year (2)
    - Rookie-of–the-Year (2)
    - Will-to-Win (2)

<u>End of Season Conference Awards:</u>
- All-Conference honor – awarded by the North Central Kentucky Cross Country Conference.

End of Season County Awards:
- All-County teams – awarded to top middle school and varsity runners in Jefferson County selected by a committee of coaches.
- All-County Academic team – earned by runners who are on the varsity regional team and have a 3.500gpa or higher. Honorable mention status is determined by the coach.

End of Season State Awards:
- All-State teams – awarded to top middle school and varsity runners in Jefferson County selected by a committee of coaches.
- All-State Academic team – awarded to runners who have been ranked in the top 25 through the season or finish in the top 25 at state and who have a 3.750gpa (3.500 for honorable mention).

Academic Awards. Academic excellence was an important part of the Cross Country programs at the J. Graham Brown School and at Shawnee High School. Several varsity awards were given at the state and county level to recognize outstanding academic achievement by athletes.

Sports Celebration

The Brown School Fall Sports Celebration was held in the auditorium on Thursday, November 18, 2004. Student-Athletes from all the fall sports were recognized. The Cross Country team was placed last in the order. I was displeased when most of the members of the first team to be recognized left the celebration before the other teams were recognized. Our presentation was rushed and did not appropriately reflect the contributions and accomplishments of the Cross Country team. It may be best for Cross Country to have its own celebration.

11 THE 2001 SEASON AT BROWN SCHOOL

Saint Xavier Tiger Run, August 25, 2001

Runner - Boys	Race	Distance	Time	Place	Out of...
Robert Halsell	Varsity	5K	18:06.10	56th	231

Runner - Boys	Race	Distance	Time	Place	Out of...
William Slider	Freshman	4K	17:55.60	44th	73

Runner - Boys	Race	Distance	Time	Place	Out of...
Price Matthews	Middle	2K	7:29.01	12th	218
Max Joslyn	Middle	2K	7:48.02	28th	218
Eric Jeter	Middle	2K	8:06.79	45th	218
Aaron Ray	Middle	2K	9:37.80	172nd	218
Peter Voelker	Middle	2K	9:52.87	183rd	218
Austin Pegram	Middle	2K	11:07.65	212th	218
TEAM	Middle	2K		14th	38

Runner - Girls	Race	Distance	Time	Place	Out of...
Meagan Geary	Middle	1 mile	9:19.30	118th	126

South Oldham Dragon Invitational, September 8, 2001

Runner - Boys	Race	Distance	Time	Place	Out of...
Robert Halsell	Varsity	5K	19:08.0	15th	127

Runner - Boys	Race	Distance	Time	Place	Out of...
William Slider	JV	5K	23:58.0	37th	93

Runner - Boys	Race	Distance	Time	Place	Out of...
Max Joslyn	Middle	1 mile	7:31.4	45th	145
Aaron Ray	Middle	1 mile	8:09.5	72nd	145
Tim Blunk	Middle	1 mile	8:36.7	99th	145

Runner - Boys	Race	Distance	Time	Place	Out of...
Eric Jeter	Elementary	1 mile	7:14.7	3rd	68
Austin Pegram	Elementary	1 mile	9:09.1	26th	68

Runner - Girls	Race	Distance	Time	Place	Out of...
Meagan Geary	Middle	1 mile	10:31.3	45th	61

Trinity and Valkyrie Invitationals, September 15, 2001

Runner - Boys	Race	Distance	Time	Place	Out of...
Robert Halsell	Varsity	5K	17:13	67th	255

Runner - Boys	Race	Distance	Time	Place	Out of...
William Slider	Freshman	4K	16:43	34th	63

Runner - Boys	Race	Distance	Time	Place	Out of...
Max Joslyn	Middle	2K	7:51	39th	238
Eric Jeter	Middle	2K	7:51	40th	238
Aaron Ray	Middle	2K	8:56	121st	238
Peter Voelker	Middle	2K	11:49	236th	238
Tim Blunk	Middle	2K	11:59	237th	238
Gary Morton	Middle	2K	15:25	238th	238
TEAM	Middle	2K		13th	26

Runner - Girls	Race	Distance	Time	Place	Out of...
Meagan Geary	Middle	2K	10:08	90th	131

DeSales Invitational, October 13, 2001

Runner - Boys	Race	Distance	Time	Place	Out of...
William Slider	Varsity	5K	21:49.30	40th	58
Price Matthews	Varsity	5K	27:24.04	54th	58
Max Joslyn	Varsity	5K	28:22.78	55th	58
Mike Taylor	Varsity	5K	28:24.35	56th	58
Aaron Ray	Varsity	5K	28:34.00	57th	58
TEAM	Varsity	5K		7th	7

Jefferson County Public Schools Championship, October 16, 2001

Runner - Boys	Race	Distance	Time	Place	Out of...
William Slider	Varsity	5K	21:12.88	47th	79
Max Joslyn	Varsity	5K	24:34.94	73rd	79
Eric Jeter	Varsity	5K	25:42.19	75th	79
Mike Taylor	Varsity	5K	26:33.63	76th	79
Aaron Ray	Varsity	5K	26:34.10	77th	79
TEAM	Varsity	5K		10th	12[137]

The Meet of Champions,[138] October 20, 2001

Runner - Boys	Race	Distance	Time	Place	Out of...
Robert Halsell	Varsity	5K	17:50.5	12th	146
William Slider	Varsity	5K	21:34.7	106th	146

Runner - Boys	Race	Distance	Time	Place	Out of...
Eric Jeter	Elementary	3K	12:55.3	15th	72

Runner - Girls	Race	Distance	Time	Place	Out of...
Meagan Geary	Elementary	3K	17:04.9	46th	65

---

[137] Only twelve of the twenty-four Jefferson County Public Schools fielded full teams.

[138] The Meet of Champions is also the state championship for elementary and middle school runners.

Region 2 Class A Meet, October 27, 2001

Runner - Boys	Race	Distance	Time	Place	Out of...
Robert Halsell	Varsity	5K	17:02.3	6th	
William Slider	Varsity	5K	19:46.1	43rd	64
Price Matthews	Varsity	5K	21:47.9	55th	64
Eric Jeter	Varsity	5K	22:29.4	58th	64
Aaron Ray	Varsity	5K	22:47.0	59th	64
TEAM	Varsity	5K		7th	64

Class A State Meet, November 3, 2001

Runner - Boys	Race	Distance	Time	Place	Out of...
Robert Halsell	Varsity	5K	17:23.4	17th	205

12 THE 2002 SEASON AT BROWN SCHOOL

Saint Xavier Tiger Run, August 30, 2002

Runner - Boys	Race	Distance	Time	Place	Out of...
Robert Halsell	Varsity	5K	17:05.32	34th	302
William Slider	Varsity	5K	21:03.02	210th	302
Josh Chervenak	Varsity	5K	26:01.41	277th	302

Runner - Boys	Race	Distance	Time	Place	Out of...
Blake Braden	Middle	2K	8:18.09	65th	301
Max Joslyn	Middle	2K	9:23.53	112th	301
Eric Jeter	Middle	2K	11:07.97	163rd	301
David Read	Middle	2K	12:58.73	180th	301
Tim Blunk	Middle	2K	16:14.71	198th	301
TEAM	Middle	2K		24th	40

Runner - Girls	Race	Distance	Time	Place	Out of...
Krysta Lathon	Middle	2K	10:29.89	155th	229
Mary Tanner	Middle	2K	13:38.45	226th	229

Male Invitational, September 7, 2002

Runner - Boys	Race	Distance	Time	Place	Out of...
Robert Halsell	Varsity	5K	17:59	2nd	92
William Slider	JV	4K	15:15	12th	108
Blake Braden	JV	4K	17:56	71st	108
Max Joslyn	JV	4K	19:22	95th	108

South Oldham Dragon Invitational, September 14, 2002

Runner - Boys	Race	Distance	Time	Place	Out of...
Robert Halsell	Varsity	5K	18:29.49	20th	124
William Slider	JV	5K	21:57.21	38th	94

Runner - Boys	Race	Distance	Time	Place	Out of...
Aaron Ray	Middle	1 mile	7:08.83	37th	171
Blake Braden	Middle	1 mile	7:15.43	45th	171
Eric Jeter	Middle	1 mile	7:50.34	93rd	171
Max Joslyn	Middle	1 mile	7:57.45	101st	171
David Read	Middle	1 mile	8:09.00	114th	171
Tim Blunk	Middle	1 mile	8:26.23	124th	171
Nick Logsdon	Middle	1 mile	8:38.02	132nd	171
Brian Valentine	Middle	1 mile	8:41.57	135th	171
Dominique Oliver	Middle	1 mile	9:52.64	167th	171
Team	Middle	1 mile		12th	16

Runner - Girls	Race	Distance	Time	Place	Out of...
Krysta Lathon	Elementary	1 mile	8:28.27	12th	111
Mary Tanner	Elementary	1 mile	10:52.10	81st	111
Chelsae Lathon	Middle	1 mile	9:54.03	100th	113

Trinity Invitational, September 21, 2002

Runner - Boys	Race	Distance	Time	Place	Out of...
Robert Halsell	Varsity	5K	16:53.01	26th	167

Runner - Boys	Race	Distance	Time	Place	Out of...
Aaron Ray	Middle	2K	9:42	57th	278
Blake Braden	Middle	2K	9:45	61st	278
Tim Blunk	Middle	2K	10:27	121st	278
Eric Jeter	Middle	2K	10:39	147th	278
David Read	Middle	2K	10:40	150th	278
Max Joslyn	Middle	2K	10:40	151st	278
Austin Pegram	Middle	2K	11:43	215th	278
Nick Logsdon	Middle	2K	12:10	230th	278
Brian Valentine	Middle	2K	12:12	231st	278
Isaac Poole	Middle	2K	13:48	261st	278
Shelby Dixon	Middle	2K	14:13	265th	278
Griffith Williams	Middle	2K	14:40	269th	278
TEAM	Middle	2K		16th	37

Sacred Heart Valkyrie Invitational, September 21, 2002

Runner - Girls	Race	Distance	Time	Place	Out of...
Krysta Lathon	Middle	2K	10:41	40th	196
Chelsae Lathon	Middle	2K	12:14	125th	196
Mary Tanner	Middle	2K	14:32	189th	196

Rocket Relays, October 5, 2002

Runners - Boys	Race	Distance	Time	Place	Out of ...
William Slider, Aaron Ray, Rob Halsell	Varsity	3x3K	33:58	5th	17
Blake Braden, Tim Blunk, Max Joslyn	Varsity	3x3K	40:25	14th	17
Eric Jeter, David Read, Brian Valentine	Varsity	3x3K	43:08	15th	17

DeSales Invitational, October 19, 2002

Runner - Boys	Race	Distance	Time	Place	Out of...
Rob Halsell	Varsity	5K	17:32.0	5th	133
William Slider	Varsity	5K	20:17.0	81st	133

Runner - Boys	Race	Distance	Time	Place	Out of...
Blake Braden	Middle	4K	16:51	26th	78
David Read	Middle	4K	17:54	37th	78
Griffith Williams	Middle	4K	18:01	38th	78
Max Joslyn	Middle	4K	18:12	43rd	78
Tim Blunk	Middle	4K	18:21	48th	78
Eric Jeter	Middle	4K	18:29	53rd	78
Nick Logsdon	Middle	4K	20:00	66th	78
Brian Valentine	Middle	4K	21:19	73rd	78
Isaac Poole	Middle	4K	26:22	77th	78
Shelby Dixon	Middle	4K	28:38	78th	78
Team	Middle	4K		5th	5

Runner - Girls	Race	Distance	Time	Place	Out of ...
Krysta Lathon	JV	5K	25:32.0	19th	52
Chelsae Lathon	Middle	4K	24:27.0	44th	46

Jefferson County Public Schools Championship, October 22, 2002

Runner - Boys	Race	Distance	Time	Place	Out of...
Rob Halsell	Varsity	5K	17:30.82	2nd	89
William Slider	Varsity	5K	20:31.83	44th	89
David Read	Varsity	5K	23:39.99	70th	89
Aaron Ray	Varsity	5K	24:06.30	72nd	89
Tim Blunk	Varsity	5K	24:08.55	73rd	89
Eric Jeter	Varsity	5K	24:49.56	76th	89
Max Joslyn	Varsity	5K	25:57.14	79th	89
TEAM	Varsity	5K		9th	14[139]

Runner – Girls	Race	Distance	Time	Place	Out of ...
Krysta Lathon	Varsity	5K	26:06.61	33rd	58

Metro Meet of Champions, October 27, 2002

Runner – Boys	Race	Distance	Time	Place	Out of ...
Rob Halsell	Varsity	5K	16:40	13th	198
William Slider	Varsity	5K	20:11	145th	198
Eric Jeter	Varsity	5K	21:56	171st	198
Aaron Ray	Varsity	5K	22:56	185th	198
Blake Braden	Varsity	5K	23:07	186th	198
Tim Blunk	Varsity	5K	24:50	193rd	198
David Read	Varsity	5K	24:58	195th	198
Nick Logsdon	Varsity	5K	25:53	198th	198
Team	Varsity	5K		20th	24

Runner – Girls	Race	Distance	Time	Place	Out of ...
Krysta Lathon	Varsity	5K	25:19	81st	106

[139] Only fourteen of the twenty-four Jefferson County Public Schools fielded any runners.

Region 2 Class A Meet, November 2, 2002

Runner - Boys	Race	Distance	Time	Place	Out of...
Robert Halsell	Varsity	5K	17:55.65	3rd	61
William Slider	Varsity	5K	20:27.81	29th	61
Eric Jeter	Varsity	5K	22:33.09	51st	61
Blake Braden	Varsity	5K	22:53.84	52nd	61
David Read	Varsity	5K	22:57.33	53rd	61
Aaron Ray	Varsity	5K	24:18.15	59th	61
Tim Blunk	Varsity	5K	24:43.29	61st	61
TEAM	Varsity	5K		8th	8

Runner - Girls	Race	Distance	Time	Place	Out of...
Krysta Lathon	Varsity	5K	25:02.07	22nd	44

Class A State Meet, November 9, 2002

Runner - Boys	Race	Distance	Time	Place	Out of...
Robert Halsell	Varsity	5K	17:11.13	9th	206

13 THE 2003 BROWN SCHOOL SEASON

Saint Xavier Tiger Run, August 30, 2003

Runner - Boys	Race	Distance	Time	Place	Out of...
Robert Halsell	Varsity	5K	No Time[140]	34th	262
William Slider	Varsity	5K	No Time	168th	262
Josh Chervenak	Varsity	5K	No Time	209th	262

Runner - Boys	Race	Distance	Time	Place	Out of...
Eric Jeter	Middle	2K	8:05	45th	223
Jordan Smith	Middle	2K	8:13	57th	223
Tim Blunk	Middle	2K	8:23	70th	223
David Read	Middle	2K	8:31	83rd	223
Brian Valentine	Middle	2K	9:22	146th	223
Nick Logsdon	Middle	2K	9:23	147th	223
Isaac Poole	Middle	2K	11:05	210th	223
TEAM[141]	Middle	2K			

Runner - Girls	Race	Distance	Time	Place	Out of...
Kelly McRoberts	Middle	2K	7:49.09	6th	199
Krysta Lathon	Middle	2K	9:43.45	82nd	199
Maddie Dailey	Middle	2K	9:58.72	102nd	199
Sami Siegwald	Middle	2K	10:10.44	115th	199
TEAM	Middle	2K		16th	31

---

[140] Times for the Boys Varsity Race were not reported.
[141] No Team Scores were reported for the Middle School Boys.

South Oldham Dragon Invitational, September, 2003

Runner - Boys	Race	Distance	Time	Place	Out of...
Robert Halsell	Varsity	5K	19:15.73	18th	124
William Slider	Varsity	5K	21:58.09	81st	124
Josh Chervenak	Varsity	5K	22:40.18	89th	124

Runner - Boys	Race	Distance	Time	Place	Out of...
Eric Jeter	Middle	1 mile	6:07.49	21st	159
Jordan Smith	Middle	1 mile	6:18.70	27th	159
Zach Torp	Middle	1 mile	6:26.72	43rd	159
Tim Blunk	Middle	1 mile	6:27.43	44th	159
Brian Valentine	Middle	1 mile	6:44.47	59th	159
Cameron Carter	Middle	1 mile	7:52.24	131st	159
Griffith Williams	Middle	1 mile	8:18.76	142nd	159
Dominique Oliver	Middle	1 mile	8:36.28	148th	159
TEAM	Middle	1 mile		4th	16

Runner - Girls	Race	Distance	Time	Place	Out of...
Kelly McRoberts	Middle	1 mile	6:05.97	4th	169
Sami Siegwald	Middle	1 mile	7:23.64	49th	169
Krysta Lathon	Middle	1 mile	7:26.17	51st	169
Erica Stoddard	Middle	1 mile	7:53.12	82nd	169
Maddie Dailey	Middle	1 mile	8:13.94	107th	169
Mary Walker	Middle	1 mile	10:10.31	156th	169
TEAM	Middle	1 mile		10th	18

Trinity Invitational, September 20, 2003[142]

Runner - Boys	Race	Distance	Time	Place	Out of...
Robert Halsell	Varsity	5K	17:50.33	66th	273
William Slider	Varsity	5K	20:19.06	192nd	273
Josh Chervenak	Varsity	5K	21:24.30	228th	273
Aaron Ray	Varsity	5K	22:52.38	259th	273

---

[142] Middle School results were not reported.

Runner - Boys	Race	Distance	Time	Place	Out of...
Eric Jeter	Middle	2.5K	11:11.06	32nd	259
Jordan Smith	Middle	2.5K	11:22.76	45th	259
David Read	Middle	2.5K	11:49.20	69th	259
Brian Valentine	Middle	2.5K	11:57.18	84th	259
Tim Blunk	Middle	2.5K	11:57.55	85th	259
Nick Logsdon	Middle	2.5K	13:00.10	140th	259
Griffith Williams	Middle	2.5K	14:14.94	204th	259
TEAM	Middle	2.5K		10th	27

Runner - Girls	Race	Distance	Time	Place	Out of...
Kelly McRoberts	Middle	2.5K	12:01.90	18th	220
Sami Siegwald	Middle	2.5K	13:19.94	73rd	220
Krysta Lathon	Middle	2.5K	13:23.35	75th	220
Mary Walker	Middle	2.5K	14:08.56	115th	220
Eric Stoddard	Middle	2.5K	14:13.09	119th	220
TEAM	Middle	2.5K		13th	25

North Central Kentucky Cross Country Conference, October 18th, 2003

Runner - Boys	Race	Distance	Time	Place	Out of...
Rob Halsell	Varsity	5K	17:31.95	2nd	67
William Slider	Varsity	5K	19:59.89	38th	67
Tim Blunk	Varsity	5K	20:29.78	42nd	67
Eric Jeter	Varsity	5K	20:39.53	44th	67
Josh Chervenak	Varsity	5K	21:30.08	52nd	67
David Read	Varsity	5K	21:38.20	54th	67
Nick Logsdon	Varsity	5K	24:03.94	66th	67
Brian Valentine	Varsity	5K	26:24.55	67th	67
TEAM	Varsity	5K		7th	9

Runner - Girls	Race	Distance	Time	Place	Out of ...
Kelly McRoberts	Varsity	5K	20:32.61	2nd	54
Krysta Lathon	Varsity	5K	23:54.72	29th	54
Maddie Dailey	Varsity	5K	24:15.06	31st	54
Erica Stoddard	Varsity	5K	25:19.26	41st	54
Sami Siegwald	Varsity	5K	26:17.59	47th	54
TEAM	Varsity	5K		6th	8

Meet of Champions and Elementary and Middle School State Championships, October 25th, 2003

Runner – Boys	Race	Distance	Time	Place	Out of ...
William Slider	Varsity	5K	21:01.54	56th	122

Runner – Boys	Race	Distance	Time	Place	Out of ...
Eric Jeter	Middle	4K	16:15.13	67th	325
David Read	Middle	4K	17:28.29	134th	325
Jordan Smith	Middle	4K	18:09.17	183rd	325
Tim Blunk	Middle	4K	18:16.10	191st	325
Brian Valentine	Middle	4K	19:11.58	229th	325
TEAM	Middle	4K		26th	34

Runner – Boys	Race	Distance	Time	Place	Out of ...
Clay McRoberts	Elementary	3K	13:14.34	51st	252

Runner – Girls	Race	Distance	Time	Place	Out of ...
Kelly McRoberts	Middle	4K	17:22.25	22nd	253
Krysta Lathon	Middle	4K	19:41.37	125th	253
Maddie Dailey	Middle	4K	19:43.95	131st	253
Sami Siegwald	Middle	4K	20:20.33	154th	253
Erica Stoddard	Middle	4K	23:01.85	218th	253
TEAM	Middle	4K		20th	27

Region 2 Class A Meet, November 1, 2003

Runner - Boys	Race	Distance	Time	Place	Out of ...
Robert Halsell	Varsity	5K	17:15.42	1st	61
Eric Jeter	Varsity	5K	20:06.15	29th	61
William Slider	Varsity	5K	20:48.74	42nd	61
Jordan Smith	Varsity	5K	21:36.65	48th	61
Tim Blunk	Varsity	5K	21:57.93	49th	61
David Read	Varsity	5K	22:00.71	50th	61
Zach Torp	Varsity	5K	22:10.50	53rd	61
TEAM	Varsity	5K		7th	8

Runner - Girls	Race	Distance	Time	Place	Out of ...
Kelly McRoberts	Varsity	5K	21:17.65	3rd	44

Krysta Lathon	Varsity	5K	24:11.60	20th	44
Maddie Dailey	Varsity	5K	24:27.45	21st	44
Sami Siegwald	Varsity	5K	25:27.25	28th	44
Erica Stoddard	Varsity	5K	26:56.77	39th	44
TEAM[143]	Varsity	5K		5th	7

Class A State Meet, November 8, 2003

Runner - Boys	Race	Distance	Time	Place	Out of...
Robert Halsell[144]	Varsity	5K	17:18.32	10th	196

Runner - Girls	Race	Distance	Time	Place	Out of...
Kelly McRoberts	Varsity	5K	21:13.22	21st	183
Krysta Lathon	Varsity	5K	23:36.90	89th	183
Maddie Dailey	Varsity	5K	25:28.88	143rd	183

---

[143] The girls team finished two points out of fourth place and missed qualifying as a team for state.

[144] Rob Halsell received the Sportsmanship Trophy for the state meet.

14 THE 2004 BROWN SCHOOL SEASON

The 2004 Cross Country season at the Brown School was different in many respects. We no long had our dominant runner, Rob Halsell. We would need to replace Rob with a pack-running mentality.

My son, William Slider, not only took over as the team captain and lead runner, but also as the Middle School coach. These added responsibilities placed a great deal of emotional stress on William, but he responded very well. Without William, the team would never have been successful.

Also, in anticipation of our regional meet being held at a difficult course, I scheduled many of our meets on that course or other difficult ones. This decision did hurt some of the runners' times during the season – especially the more muscular runners like William – but these racing experiences on difficult terrain prepared the team for success at the region.

I give more detail for each of these meets to give the reader an idea of the specific challenges for both the coaches and the athletes. Each meet had its own story for every runner.

Saint Xavier Tiger Run, September 4, 2004

We entered sixteen runners at a cost of $80 ($5 per runner). Fees were paid by the Brown School Bear Runners. This meet was traditionally the first of the season for Brown School. The weather was increasingly hot and humid with no wind. The course, Seneca Park, had good footing. Seneca Park was always a fast course with only one hill to negotiate. It is no longer used for high school meets.

Runner - Boys	Race	Distance	Time	Place	Out of...
William Slider	Varsity	5K	20:21.08	174th	239
Josh Chervenak	Varsity	5K	22:27.55	217th	239
Tim Blunk	Varsity	5K	DNF		

Runner - Boys	Race	Distance	Time	Place	Out of...
Eric Jeter	Middle	2K	7:59.09	32nd	286
Jordan Smith	Middle	2K	8:08.77	47th	286
Clay McRoberts	Middle	2K	8:26.71	79th	286
Isaac Poole	Middle	2K	8:38.17	96th	286
David Read	Middle	2K	8:38.71	97th	286
Griffith Williams	Middle	2K	9:27.48	171st	286
Shelby Dixon	Middle	2K	9:59.49	214th	286
Jay Connelly	Middle	2K	10:10.79	222nd	286
Houston Ward	Middle	2K	10:24.38	233rd	286
Zach Torp	Middle	2K	DNR		
TEAM	Middle	2K		13th	33

Runner - Girls	Race	Distance	Time	Place	Out of...
Kelly McRoberts	Varsity	5K	21:41.70	30th	185
Maddie Dailey	Middle	2K	8:42.49	42nd	201
Sami Siegwald	Middle	2K	9:12.60	62nd	201

Male Invitational, September 11, 2004[145]

We entered 12 runners at a cost of $57 ($4.75 per runner). Fees were paid by me. I liked this race because of the 4K distance for JV runners. I only ran William Slider in the varsity race and formed a JV team with Josh Chervenak as the team captain. The weather was increasingly hot and humid with no wind. The course had good footing, but it is very challenging with a long hill to negotiate. This park, however, was where the team practiced some there was some "home field" advantage.

Runner - Boys	Race	Distance	Time	Place	Out of...
William Slider	Varsity	5K	20:56	46th	80

---

[145] JV results were not reported.

Runner - Boys	Race	Distance	Time	Place	Out of...
Eric Jeter	JV	4K	15:15.40	15th	
Tim Blunk	JV	4K	16:03		
Josh Chervenak	JV	4K	16:30		
Jordan Smith	JV	4K	16:59		
Zach Torp	JV	4K	17:04		
Isaac Poole	JV	4K	17:28		
David Read	JV	4K	DNF		
Clay McRoberts	JV	4K	DNR		

Runner - Girls	Race	Distance	Time	Place	Out of...
Kelly McRoberts	Varsity	5K	23:04	5th	67
Maddie Dailey	JV	4K	18:24	16th	
Sami Siegwald	JV	4K	20:00	31st	

Trinity and Valkyrie Invitationals, September 18, 2004[146]

We entered 16 runners at a cost of $65 ($4.06 per runner). Fees were paid by me. This was a nice, big local meet on a fairly fast course. Weather was dry, but comfortable through the morning, but got progressively hotter.

I decided to give Kelly McRoberts some exposure to a high level varsity meet. She responded very well.

Runner - Boys	Race	Distance	Time	Place	Out of...
William Slider	Varsity	5K	19:59.37	137th	202
Josh Chervenak	Varsity	5K	22:27.70	188th	202
Tim Blunk	Freshman	5K	21:27.43	35th	

Runner - Boys	Race	Distance	Time	Place	Out of...
Eric Jeter	Middle	2.5K	10:37.63	13th	
Isaac Poole	Middle	2.5K	11:42.65	68th	
Griffith Williams	Middle	2.5K	11:44.46	70th	
David Read	Middle	2.5K	12:06.02	91st	
Jay Connelly	Middle	2.5K	13:24.56	175th	
Houston Ward	Middle	2.5K	14:15.37	218th	
Jordan Smith	Middle	2.5K	DNF		
Shelby Dixon	Middle	2.5K	DNR		
Clay McRoberts	Middle	2.5K	DNR		
Zach Torp	Middle	2.5K	DNR		
TEAM	Middle	2.5K		15th	37

---

[146] Middle School results were not reported.

Runner - Girls	Race	Distance	Time	Place	Out of...
Kelly McRoberts	Varsity	5K	22:06.52	68th	190
Maddie Dailey	Middle	2.5K	12:40.16	36th	
Sami Siegwald	Middle	2.5K	14:08.30	76th	

Jefferson County Public Middle School Region 2 Championships, September 20, 2004

This meet was a good showcase for our middle school runners. Thirteen runners were entered at a cost of $25 ($1.92 per runner). Fees were paid by the director of athletics. The weather was dry, but comfortable. The course at Creason Park was flat.

William Slider as the Middle School coach ran the team completely. I was there for administrative support and for liability requirements. William was in charge and worked hard.

Runner - Boys	Race	Distance	Time	Place	Out of...
Clay McRoberts	6th	½ mile	2:46	3rd	
Houston Ward	6th	½ mile	3:07	18th	
Isaac Poole	7th	1 mile	5:50	8th	
Griffith Williams	7th	1 mile	6:03	12th	
Jay Connelly	7th	1 mile	6:37		
Shelby Dixon	7th	1 mile	6:56		
Eric Jeter	8th	1 mile	5:14	1st	
Jordan Smith	8th	1 mile	5:48	3rd	
David Read	8th	1 mile	8:03	10th	
Zach Torp	8th	1 mile	DNR		

Runner - Girls	Race	Distance	Time	Place	Out of...
Sami Siegwald	7th	1 mile	6:43	4th	
Kelly McRoberts	8th	1 mile	5:48	1st	
Maddie Dailey	8th	1 mile	6:20	3rd	

Shively Freshman Championships, September 23, 2004

This meet was another good opportunity for the Middle School runners and their coach. Results were never published and the distance not accurate. Seventeen runners were entered at a cost of $75 ($4.42 per runner) and paid by Brown School Bear Runners. The weather was dry and hot.

Runner - Boys	Race	Distance	Time	Place	Out of...
Tim Blunk	Frosh	2 mile			
Eric Jeter	7/8th Grade	1 mile		3rd	
David Read	7/8th	1 mile			
Jordan Smith	7/8th	1 mile			
Isaac Poole	7/8th	1 mile			
Griffith Williams	7/8th	1 mile			
Jay Connelly	7/8th	1 mile			
Shelby Dixon	7/8th	1 mile			
Zach Torp	7/8th	1 mile			
Clay McRoberts	3/6th	1 mile		2nd	
Houston Ward	3/6th	1 mile			
Raleigh Dixon	3/6th	1 mile			
TEAM	7/8th	1 mile		3rd	

Runner - Girls	Race	Distance	Time	Place	Out of...
Kelly McRoberts	7/8th	1 mile		4th	
Maddie Dailey	7/8th	1 mile			
Sami Siegwald	7/8th	1 mile			
Ayanna Jeter	3/6th	1 mile			

Atherton Invitational, October 2, 2004

This meet was low-key, local, and on a hilly course to begin our hill race training. Nineteen runners were entered at a cost of $85 ($4.47 per runner), which was paid by Brown School Bear Runners. The weather was dry and warming through the day. The course was a hilly, one mile loop on the school's campus.

Runner - Boys	Race	Distance	Time	Place	Out of...
William Slider	Varsity	5K	20:10.19	9th	24
Tim Blunk	Varsity	5K	21:57.48	17th	24
Josh Chervenak	Varsity	5K	22:10.19	20th	24
Clay McRoberts	Varsity	5k	22:10.66	21st	24
Isaac Poole	Varsity	5K	23:32.70	23rd	24
Zach Torp	Varsity	5K	DNF		
David Read	Varsity	5K	DNF		
Eric Jeter	Varsity	5K	DNR		
Jordan Smith	Varsity	5K	DNR		
Griffith Williams	Varsity	5K	DNR		
TEAM	Varsity	5K		4th	4

Runner - Boys	Race	Distance	Time	Place	Out of...
Jay Connelly	Middle	3K	14:40.02	18th	29
Houston Ward	Middle	3K	15:00.21	23rd	29
Shelby Dixon	Middle	3K	15:17.60	24th	29
Raleigh Dixon	Open	1 mile	9:19	1st	

Runner - Girls	Race	Distance	Time	Place	Out of...
Kelly McRoberts	Varsity	5K	22:10.72	2nd	16
Sami Siegwald	Varsity	5K	DNR		
Ayanna Jeter	Open	1 mile	DNR		

Assumption Rocket Relays, October 9, 2004

This unique competition is a different meet that allowed me to get a high school meet at a short distance for many of our younger runners. Fifteen runners were entered at a cost of $70 ($4.67 per runner), which was paid by Brown School Bear Runners. Weather was warm and dry and the course was flat and fast.

Runner - Boys	Race	Distance	Time	Place	Out of...
Tim Blunk, Eric Jeter, William Slider	Varsity	3x3K	11:21 + 10:44 + 10:56 = 33:01.1	4th	
Josh Chervenak, Isaac Poole, Clay McRoberts	Varsity	3x3K	11:48 + 11:51 + 11:49 = 35:28.7	12th	
Griffith Williams, David Read, Jay Connelly	Varsity	3x3K	12:18 + 13:07 + 15:02 = 40:27.5	15th	

Runner - Girls	Race	Distance	Time	Place	Out of...
Kelly McRoberts, Maddie Dailey, Sami Siegwald	Varsity	3 x 3K	12:02 + 12:58 + 14:19 = 39:19.9	5th	

North Central Kentucky Cross Country Conference, October 16, 2004

We joined this conference in 2003, and it was a good experience. Thirteen runners were entered at a cost of $100 ($7.69 per runner. The fee was paid by Brown School Bear Runners. The weather was cool, wet, and windy. The course was very difficult.

Runner - Boys	Race	Distance	Time	Place	Out of...
William Slider	Varsity	5K	21:23	18th	
Eric Jeter	Varsity	5K	22:11	24th	
Clay McRoberts	Varsity	5K	23:12	37th	
Tim Blunk	Varsity	5K	23:14	38th	
Zach Torp	Varsity	5K	24:12	45th	
David Read	Varsity	5K	24:42	48th	
Isaac Poole	Varsity	5K	25:17	51st	
Josh Chervenak	Varsity	5K	25:25	53rd	
Griffith Williams	Varsity	5K	26:20	59th	
TEAM	Varsity	5K		6th	

Runner - Girls	Race	Distance	Time	Place	Out of ...
Shelby Dixon	JV	5K	29:57	21st	
Jay Connelly	JV	5K	31:12	24th	
Houston Ward	JV	5K	31:23	25th	

Runner - Girls	Race	Distance	Time	Place	Out of ...
Kelly McRoberts	Varsity	5K	23:13	3rd	
Sami Siegwald	Varsity	5K	DNF		

The DeSales Invitational, October 23, 2004

This site of this meet was McNeeley Lake Park. This meet was selected because it is the site of the 2004 regionals. Fifteen runners were entered at a cost of $99 ($6.60 per runner), which was paid by Brown School Bear Runners. The weather was cool, rainy, and windy. The course was hilly and very slick. Runners without spikes were falling.

Runner - Boys	Race	Distance	Time	Place	Out of ...
William Slider	Varsity	5K	20:21	73rd	138
Eric Jeter	Varsity	5K	20:33	78th	138
Tim Blunk	Varsity	5K	20:53	90th	138
Clay McRoberts	Varsity	5K	21:15	101st	138
David Read	Varsity	5K	21:38	110th	138
Zach Torp	Varsity	5K	22:10	117th	138
Josh Chervenak	Varsity	5K	22:34	119th	138
TEAM	Varsity	5K		16th	20

Runner - Boys	Race	Distance	Time	Place	Out of ...
Griffith Williams	JV	5K	24:59	85th	94
Houston Ward	JV	5K	DNF		
Shelby Dixon	JV	5K	DNR		
Jay Connelly	JV	5K	DNR		
Isaac Poole	JV	5K	DNR		

Runner - Girls	Race	Distance	Time	Place	Out of ...
Kelly McRoberts	Varsity	5K	22:12	6th	64
Maddie Dailey	Varsity	5K	24:50	31st	64
Sami Siegwald	Varsity	5K	26:14	40th	64

Jefferson County Public Schools Varsity Championships, October 26, 2004

This meet is always a nice race on our practice course. In 2004 the championships were our only meet on Tuesday. Twelve runners were entered at a cost of $35 ($2.92 per runner), which was paid by Brown School Bear Runners. The weather was very comfortable and the course was good.

Runner - Boys	Race	Distance	Time	Place	Out of ...
William Slider	Varsity	5K	20:20	59th	115
Eric Jeter	Varsity	5K	20:21	60th	115
Tim Blunk	Varsity	5K	21:28	83rd	115
Clay McRoberts	Varsity	5K	21:55	89th	115
Josh Chervenak	Varsity	5K	22:11	92nd	115
David Read	Varsity	5K	22:11	93rd	115
Zach Torp	Varsity	5K	22:43	94th	115
Isaac Poole	Varsity	5K	23:07	98th	115
Griffith Williams	Varsity	5K	25:21	105th	115
TEAM	Varsity	5K		12	24

Runner - Girls	Race	Distance	Time	Place	Out of …
Kelly McRoberts	Varsity	5K	21:29	9th	88
Maddie Dailey	Varsity	5K	23:58	30th	88
Sami Siegwald	Varsity	5K	27:10	59th	88

Meet of Champions and Elementary and Middle School State Championships, October 30th, 2004

This meet changed venues in 2004 to Masterson Station Park, Lexington, Kentucky. The focus of this race was the Elementary and Middle School State Championships. High School runners were entered for the workout. This meet was the third race in eight days, so a lot of rest was needed afterward. Eighteen runners were entered at a cost of $125 ($6.94 per runner), which was paid by Brown School Bear Runners. The weather was hot, rainy, and windy. The course was hilly and muddy – about one and one-half minutes slow.

This meet was William's last effort as Middle School coach. He worked very hard for his runners. He was exhausted by the time his varsity race was run.

Runner – Boys	Race	Distance	Time	Place	Out of …
Clay McRoberts	Elementary	3K	12:31.86	10th	381
Houston Ward	Elementary	3K	16:18.08	271st	381
Raleigh Dixon	Elementary	3K	21:23.28	369th	381
Tim Blunk	Varsity	5K	20:41.79	80th	180
William Slider	Varsity	5K	21:06.43	96th	180
Josh Chervenak	Varsity	5K	23:05.89	136th	180

Runner – Boys	Race	Distance	Time	Place	Out of …
Eric Jeter	Middle	4K	14:46.23	23rd	405
David Read	Middle	4K	17:08.01	170th	405
Isaac Poole	Middle	4K	17:08.80	173rd	405
Griffith Williams	Middle	4K	18:25.62	271st	405
Shelby Dixon	Middle	4K	20:42.85	329th	405
Jay Connelly	Middle	4K	DNR		
Jordan Smith	Middle	4K	DNR		
Zach Torp	Middle	4K	DNR		
TEAM	Middle	4K		28th	46

Runner – Girls	Race	Distance	Time	Place	Out of ...
Ayanna Jeter	Elementary	3K	17:30.08	191st	294
Kelly McRoberts	Middle	4K	16:30.15	15th	327
Maddie Dailey	Middle	4K	18:35.37	130th	327

Class A Region 2 Championships, November 6, 2004

The Class A Region Two Championships were held on a beautiful Saturday and run on a challenging course that was wet from rains the previous week. The weather was unseasonably warm. The girls ran at about 10:15am and the boys at about 11:00am. The meet was hosted by DeSales High School.

Sami Siegwald called in sick and did not run. We certainly missed her. She had an outside chance at making state and the course would have suited her.

Kelly McRoberts grabbed the lead early in the girls race. She was challenged by Lieve Hendren of Kentucky Country Day, who passed Kelly at the two mile mark. The KCD coach had instructed her runner that if she were not leading Kelly with one-half mile to go, then Kelly would win. Kelly regained the lead and with a strong finishing kick won the championship.

Maddie Dailey ran one of her best races of the season with a consistently strong pace through the entire race. She finished fifteenth – the fifth individual qualifier.

The boys depended on a solid team finish. Eric Jeter was the top finisher for the team, running under twenty minutes. William Slider had a difficult race in the heat, finishing behind Eric for the first time this season, but having the highest finish in any of his four regionals (a testimony to the difficulty of the course). Tim Blunk, Clay McRoberts, and Zach Torp finished as a pack. Josh Chervenak and David Read bumped several runners from other teams.

I had analyzed the boys regional the week before the race. The top three schools would not be touched. The race would be for fourth place – and there were five teams that could easily take fourth. Our solid team finish gave the Brown School fourth place with room to spare. We qualified for state!

Runner – Girls	Race	Distance	Time	Place	Out of ...
Kelly McRoberts	Varsity	5K	21:42.30	1st	
Maddie Dailey	Varsity	5K	23:50.00	15th	

Runner – Boys	Race	Distance	Time	Place	Out of ...
Eric Jeter	Varsity	5K	19:51.30	12th	
William Slider	Varsity	5K	20:43.50	24th	
Tim Blunk	Varsity	5K	21:21.50	32nd	
Clay McRoberts	Varsity	5K	21:32.70	35th	
Zach Torp	Varsity	5K	21:37.40	36th	
Josh Chervenak	Varsity	5K	22:48.50	45th	
David Read	Varsity	5K	22:48.50	45th	
Isaac Poole	Varsity	5K	Alternate		
TEAM	Varsity	5K		4th	9

Class A State Championship, November 13, 2004

The Class "A" State Championships were held on a beautiful, but cool, Saturday (November 13, 2004) at the Kentucky State Horse Park in Lexington. The girls ran at 9:30am and the boys ran at 10:15am.

The team was joined by former teammate Rob Halsell, who now attends Eastern Kentucky University. Rob has red-shirted for Cross Country, but will run track in the spring.

The Brown School runners competed well. Kelly McRoberts and Maddie Dailey improved their finishes from last year.

None of the boys had ever run in the state meet before. The team was seeded twenty-first and finished twentieth. The boys improved their team time by almost two minutes over the regional meet. William Slider ran his last Cross Country race under twenty minutes, leading the team.

Runner – Girls	Race	Distance	Time	Place	Out of ...
Kelly McRoberts	Varsity	5K	21:38.28	19th	194
Maddie Dailey	Varsity	5K	24:11.59	113th	194

Runner – Boys	Race	Distance	Time	Place	Out of ...
William Slider	Varsity	5K	19:58.69	105th	202
Eric Jeter	Varsity	5K	20:34.17	135th	202
Tim Blunk	Varsity	5K	20:42.75	142nd	202
Clay McRoberts	Varsity	5K	20:48.29	145th	202
Josh Chervenak	Varsity	5K	21:09.18	151st	202
Zach Torp	Varsity	5K	21:09.73	152nd	202
David Read	Varsity	5K	22:26.20	182nd	202
Isaac Poole	Varsity	5K	Alternate		
TEAM	Varsity	5K		20th	24

15 THE 2005 BROWN SCHOOL SEASON

The Brown School team for 2005 was completely changed from the pervious season. William Slider had graduated. Many of the eighth graders transferred to different schools. The challenge for me was to shape a brand new team.

Male Invitational, September 10, 2005

Runner – Boys	Race	Distance	Time	Place	Out of …
Josh Chervenak	Varsity	5K	22:39.62	47th	50

Runner – Boys	Race	Distance	Time	Place	Out of …
Clay McRoberts	JV	4K	16:02.85	32nd	
Tim Blunk	JV	4K	16:07.37	37th	
Isaac Poole	JV	4K	16:08.04	38th	
Griffith Williams	JV	4K	17:36.92	56th	
Rhys Williams	JV	4K	18:43.84	63rd	
Shelby Dixon	JV	4K	19:24.01	71st	
Jay Connelly	JV	4K	20:56.26	77th	
Aaron Morris	JV	4K	21:55.19	79th	
Zach Dettlinger	JV	4K	24:51.75	82nd	
TEAM	JV	4K		9th	

Runner – Girls	Race	Distance	Time	Place	Out of …
Sami Siegwald	JV	4K	21:50.97	43rd	
Kayla Hill	JV	4K	23:19.17	53rd	

KCD Master Meet, September 13, 2005

Runner – Boys	Race	Distance	Time	Place	Out of …
Josh Chervenak	Varsity	5K	21:10	10th	38
Tim Blunk	Varsity	5K	21:26	13th	38
Isaac Poole	Varsity	5K	21:26	14th	38
Clay McRoberts	Varsity	5K	22:00	17th	38
Jay Connelly	Varsity	5K	26:42	31st	38
Shelby Dixon	Varsity	5K	27:03	33rd	38
Gavin Curry	Varsity	5K	30:48	35th	38
Alex Haynes	Varsity	5K	32:19	36th	38
Houston Ward	Varsity	5K	32:20	37th	38
Zach Dettlinger	Varsity	5K	32:40	38th	38
TEAM	Varsity	5K		4th	4

Runner – Girls	Race	Distance	Time	Place	Out of …
Kayla Hill	Varsity	5K	32:25	30th	33

Jefferson County Public Middle School Region 2 Championships, September 19, 2005

Runner – Girls	Race	Distance	Time	Place	Out of …
Sami Siegwald	8th	1 mile	7:16.2	10th	

Runner – Boys	Race	Distance	Time	Place	Out of …
Gavin Curry	6th	½ mile	3:23.0	28th	
Houston Ward	7th	1 mile	7:36.2	25th	
Alex Haynes	7th	1 mile	7:38.8	26th	

Runner – Boys	Race	Distance	Time	Place	Out of …
Isaac Poole	8th	1 mile	5:31.0	5th	
Griffith Williams	8th	1 mile	5:56.0	14th	
Rhys Williams	8th	1 mile	6:02.0	17th	
Shelby Dixon	8th	1 mile	6:26.0	20th	
Jay Connelly	8th	1 mile	6:40.0	25th	
Zach Dettlinger	8th	1 mile	7:55.0	39th	
TEAM	8th	1 mile		3rd	

Butler Master Meet, September 20, 2005

Runner – Boys	Race	Distance	Time	Place	Out of …
Josh Chervenak	Varsity	5K	22:20	61st	89

Shively Freshman and Middle School Championships, September 21, 2005

Runner – Boys	Race	Distance	Time	Place	Out of …
Isaac Poole	Middle	1 mile	5:45	11th	
Rhys Williams	Middle	1 mile	6:29		
Shelby Dixon	Middle	1 mile	6:40		
Alex Haynes	Middle	1 mile	8:56		
Houston Ward	Middle	1 mile	9:27		
Clay McRoberts	Elementary	1 mile	6:05	2nd	
Gavin Curry	Elementary	1 mile	7:28		

KCD Master Meet, September 27, 2005

Runner – Boys	Race	Distance	Time	Place	Out of …
Tim Blunk	Varsity	5K	20:30	3rd	35
Clay McRoberts	Varsity	5K	21:17	8th	35
Josh Chervenak	Varsity	5K	21:53	10th	35
Griffith Williams	Varsity	5K	22:47	14th	35
Rhys Williams	Varsity	5K	23:04	15th	35
Isaac Poole	Varsity	5K	23:55	20th	35
Shelby Dixon	Varsity	5K	24:04	21st	35
Jay Connelly	Varsity	5K	26:08	30th	35
Gavin Curry	Varsity	5K	26:44	31st	35
Alex Haynes	Varsity	5K	31:07	33rd	35
Zach Dettlinger	Varsity	5K	31:31	34th	35
TEAM	Varsity	5K		2nd	5

Runner – Girls	Race	Distance	Time	Place	Out of …
Kayla Hill	Varsity	5K	32:08	17th	19

JCC Master Meet, October 3, 2005

Runner – Boys	Race	Distance	Time	Place	Out of ...
Tim Blunk	Varsity	5K	21:28.8	55th	
Clay McRoberts	Varsity	5K	21:30.8	56th	
Josh Chervenak	Varsity	5K	22:05.3		
Isaac Poole	Varsity	5K	23:16.5		
Griffith Williams	Varsity	5K	23:20.1		
Rhys Williams	Varsity	5K	23:39.8		
Gavin Curry	Varsity	5K	25:27.9		
Jay Connelly	Varsity	5K	26:59.5		
Shelby Dixon	Varsity	5K	29:12.9		
Alex Haynes	Varsity	5K	33:58.0		
Zach Dettlinger	Varsity	5K	35:19.6		

Holy Cross Freshman Meet, October 6, 2005

Runner – Boys	Race	Distance	Time	Place	Out of ...
Clay McRoberts	Freshman	4K	17:22.3	56th	
Isaac Poole	Freshman	4K	17:38.9		
Griffith Williams	Freshman	4K	17:48.0		
Rhys Williams	Freshman	4K	17:51.8		
Gavin Curry	Freshman	4K	20:10.0		
Jay Connelly	Freshman	4K	20:36.1		
Shelby Dixon	Freshman	4K	20:48.6		
Alex Haynes	Freshman	4K	24:37.7		
Zach Dettlinger	Freshman	4K	25:40.6		

Runner – Girls	Race	Distance	Time	Place	Out of ...
Kayla Hill	Freshman	4K	22:10.9		

McNeely Lake Master Meet, October 11, 2005

Runner – Boys	Race	Distance	Time	Place	Out of …
Clay McRoberts	Varsity	5K	20:53	41st	116
Josh Chervenak	Varsity	5K	21:21	47th	116
Isaac Poole	Varsity	5K	21:21	48th	116
Tim Blunk	Varsity	5K	22:20	58th	116
Griffith Williams	Varsity	5K	22:59	67th	116
Rhys Williams	Varsity	5K	23:31	77th	116
Shelby Dixon	Varsity	5K	25:08	89th	116
Jay Connelly	Varsity	5K	26:20	101st	116
Gavin Curry	Varsity	5K	27:07	105th	116
Alex Haynes	Varsity	5K	30:42	112th	116
Zach Dettlinger	Varsity	5K	30:45	113th	116
TEAM	Varsity	5K		8th	10

Runner – Girls	Race	Distance	Time	Place	Out of …
Kayla Hill	Varsity	5K	31:34	69th	83

Atherton Master Meet, October 18, 2005

Runner – Boys	Race	Distance	Time	Place	Out of …
Clay McRoberts	Varsity	5K	21:12		
Josh Chervenak	Varsity	5K	21:49		
Tim Blunk	Varsity	5K	21:50		
Isaac Poole	Varsity	5K	22:45		
Griffith Williams	Varsity	5K	24:40		
Rhys Williams	Varsity	5K	25:15		
Gavin Curry	Varsity	5K	26:04		
Shelby Dixon	Varsity	5K	26:36		
Alex Haynes	Varsity	5K	31:48		
Zach Dettlinger	Varsity	5K	33:17		

Male Freshman Challenge, October 25, 2005

Runner – Boys	Race	Distance	Time	Place	Out of …
Clay McRoberts	Varsity	5K	21:18		
Shelby Dixon	Varsity	5K	23:20		
Gavin Curry	Varsity	5K	26:40		
Alex Haynes	Varsity	5K	28:47		
Zach Dettlinger	Varsity	5K	29:52		

Jefferson County Public School Championship, October 25, 2005

Runner – Girls	Race	Distance	Time	Place	Out of ...
Kayla Hill	Varsity	5K	29:26	75th	84

Runner – Boys	Race	Distance	Time	Place	Out of ...
Josh Chervenak	Varsity	5K	21:55		
Clay McRoberts	Varsity	5K	21:59		
Tim Blunk	Varsity	5K	22:09		
Isaac Poole	Varsity	5K	23:11		
Griffith Williams	Varsity	5K	23:14		
Rhys Williams	Varsity	5K	23:18		
Shelby Dixon	Varsity	5K	23:35		
Gavin Curry	Varsity	5K	23:59		
Jay Connelly	Varsity	5K	25:25		
Alex Haynes	Varsity	5K	28:57		

Class A Region 2 Championship, November 5, 2005 at McNeely Lake Master Meet, October 11, 2005

Runner – Boys	Race	Distance	Time	Place	Out of ...
Isaac Poole	Varsity	5K	20:39.33	18th	61
Tim Blunk	Varsity	5K	21:37.96	28th	61
Griffith Williams	Varsity	5K	22:49.64	39th	61
Clay McRoberts	Varsity	5K	22:51.24	40th	61
Josh Chervenak	Varsity	5K	23:39.88	46th	61
Rhys Williams	Varsity	5K	24:30.05	52nd	61
Shelby Dixon	Varsity	5K	25:44.76	57th	61
TEAM	Varsity	5K		7th	8

Runner – Girls	Race	Distance	Time	Place	Out of ...
Kayla Hill	Varsity	5K	27:49.53	27th	45

16 THE 2006 SHAWNEE HIGH SCHOOL SEASON

By 2006 I was ready for a change. I was offered the opportunity to coach at Shawnee High School. I believed that this change would let me focus on high school coaching, develop a struggling program, and survey an unfamiliar area for ministry opportunities.

As the 2006 season developed I realized that there were many obstacles to overcome if I were to build and develop a team and a ministry to a neglected part of the community. I eventually came to the conclusion that I needed to step aside from coaching so that I could focus on my call to ministry. My new appointment as a pastor in 2007 was a good time to stop coaching. I enjoyed the young people whom I coached for the year, but my stepping aside allowed for the possibility of another coach having an opportunity.

JCC Master Meet, September 19, 2005

Runner – Boys	Race	Distance	Time	Place	Out of ...
Jamal Bacon	Varsity	5K	20:44		
Jordan Klunk	Varsity	5K	21:43		
Lee Bryant	Varsity	5K	22:35		
Charles Pearson	Varsity	5K	23:10		

Runner – Girls	Race	Distance	Time	Place	Out of ...
Mary Goode	Varsity	5K	28:57		

Shawnee Master Meet, September 26, 2005

Runner – Boys	Race	Distance	Time	Place	Out of …
Jamal Bacon	Varsity	5K	19:51	12th	110
Lee Bryant	Varsity	5K	20:58	27th	110
Matt Martin	Varsity	5K	21:25	28th	110
Jordan Klunk	Varsity	5K	21:42	34th	110
Charles Pearson	Varsity	5K	22:27	43rd	110
TEAM	Varsity	5K		5th	14

Runner – Girls	Race	Distance	Time	Place	Out of …
Mary Goode	Varsity	5K	30:26	50th	62

River Road Master Meet, October 3, 2005

Runner – Boys	Race	Distance	Time	Place	Out of …
Charles Pearson	Varsity	5K	21:59	62nd	108
Jordan Klunk	Varsity	5K	22:58	77th	108
Lee Bryant	Varsity	5K	28:07	107th	108

McNeely Lake Master Meet, October 10, 2005

Runner – Boys	Race	Distance	Time	Place	Out of …
Jamal Bacon	Varsity	5K	20:00.61	13th	86
Lee Bryant	Varsity	5K	22:07.30	34th	86
Jordan Klunk	Varsity	5K	22:51.06	43rd	86
Charles Pearson	Varsity	5K	22:57.20	45th	86
Matt Pasley	Varsity	5K	22:58.48	46th	86
TEAM	Varsity	5K		5th	12

Class AA Region 3, November 4, 2005

Runner – Boys	Race	Distance	Time	Place	Out of …
Lee Bryant	Varsity	5K	20:26.79	30th	62
Matt Pasley	Varsity	5K	21:44.48	47th	62
Jordan Klunk	Varsity	5K	21:56.52	48th	62

17 ROSTERS, LISTS, AND RECORDS

Alphabetical List of Runners, 2001-2006[147]

Runner – Boys	School	2001	2002	2003	2004	2005	2006
Jamal Bacon	Shawnee						X
Tim Blunk	Brown	X	X	X	X	X	
Blake Braden	Brown		X				
Lee Bryant	Shawnee						X
Cameron Carter	Brown			X			
Josh Chervenak	Brown		X	X	X	X	
Jay Connelly	Brown				X	X	
Gavin Curry	Brown					X	
Zach Dettlinger	Brown					X	
Raleigh Dixon	Brown				X	X	
Shelby Dixon	Brown		X	X	X	X	
Rob Halsell	Brown	X	X	X			
Alex Haynes	Brown					X	
Jordan Klunk	Shawnee						X
Eric Jeter	Brown	X	X	X	X		
Max Joslyn	Brown	X	X				
Nick Logsdon	Brown		X	X			
Matt Martin	Shawnee						X
Price Matthews	Brown	X					
Clay McRoberts	Brown			X	X		
Aaron Morris	Brown					X	
Gary Morton	Brown	X					

[147] X = year of running

Runner	School	2001	2002	2003	2004	2005	2006
Dominique Oliver	Brown		X	X			
Matt Pasley	Shawnee						X
Charles Pearson	Shawnee						X
Austin Pegram	Brown	X					
Isaac Poole	Brown		X	X	X	X	
Aaron Ray	Brown	X	X	X			
David Read	Brown		X	X	X		
William Slider	Brown	X	X	X	X		
Jordan Smith	Brown			X	X		
Mike Taylor	Brown	X					
Zach Torp	Brown			X	X		
Brian Valentine	Brown		X				
Peter Voelker	Brown	X					
Houston Ward	Brown				X	X	
Griffith Williams	Brown		X	X	X	X	
Rhys Williams	Brown					X	
TOTAL = 38		11	15	16	14	13	6

Runner – Girls	School	2001	2002	2003	2004	2005	2006
Meagan Geary	Brown	X					
Maddie Dailey	Brown			X	X		
Mary Goode	Shawnee						X
Kayla Hill	Brown					X	
Ayanna Jeter	Brown				X		
Chelsae Lathon	Brown		X				
Krysta Lathon	Brown		X	X			
Kelly McRoberts	Brown			X	X		
Sami Siegwald	Brown			X	X	X	
Erica Stoddard	Brown			X			
Mary Tanner	Brown		X				
Mary Walker	Brown			X			
TOTAL = 12		1	3	6	4	2	1

Top Twenty Girls 5K Times

Though most of the girls who competed for me were Middle School students, the primary races that were run in competition was the High School varsity distance – 5 Kilometers.

Rank	Runner - Girls	School	Year	Time
1	Kelly McRoberts	Brown	2003	20:32.61
2	Kelly McRoberts	Brown	2003	21:13.22

3	Kelly McRoberts	Brown	2003	21:17.65
4	Kelly McRoberts	Brown	2004	21:29.00
5	Kelly McRoberts	Brown	2004	21:38.28
6	Kelly McRoberts	Brown	2004	21:41.70
7	Kelly McRoberts	Brown	2004	21:42.30
8	Kelly McRoberts	Brown	2004	22:06.52
9	Kelly McRoberts	Brown	2004	22:10.72
10	Kelly McRoberts	Brown	2004	22:12.00
11	Kelly McRoberts	Brown	2004	23:04.00
12	Kelly McRoberts	Brown	2004	23:13.00
13	Krysta Lathon	Brown	2003	23:36.90
14	Krysta Lathon	Brown	2003	23:54.72
15	Maddie Dailey	Brown	2004	23:50.00
16	Maddie Dailey	Brown	2004	23:58.00
17	Maddie Dailey	Brown	2004	24:11.59
18	Krysta Lathon	Brown	2003	24:11.60
19	Maddie Dailey	Brown	2003	24:15.06
20	Maddie Dailey	Brown	2003	24:27.45

Top Forty Boys 5K Times

The primary distance for boys High School varsity is the 5 Kilometers. A runner had to run four High School races to qualify for regionals.

Rank	Runner - Boys	School	Year	Time
1	Robert Halsell	Brown	2002	16:40.00
2	Robert Halsell	Brown	2002	16:53.01
3	Robert Halsell	Brown	2001	17:02.30
4	Robert Halsell	Brown	2002	17:05.32
5	Robert Halsell	Brown	2002	17:11.13
6	Robert Halsell	Brown	2001	17:13.00
7	Robert Halsell	Brown	2003	17:15.42
8	Robert Halsell	Brown	2003	17:18.32
9	Robert Halsell	Brown	2001	17:23.40
10	Robert Halsell	Brown	2002	17:30.82
11	Robert Halsell	Brown	2003	17:31.95
12	Robert Halsell	Brown	2002	17:32.00
13	Robert Halsell	Brown	2003	17:50.33
14	Robert Halsell	Brown	2001	17:50.50
15	Robert Halsell	Brown	2002	17:55.65
16	Robert Halsell	Brown	2002	17:59.00
17	Robert Halsell	Brown	2001	18:06.10

18	Robert Halsell	Brown	2002	18:29.49
19	Robert Halsell	Brown	2001	19:08.00
20	Robert Halsell	Brown	2003	19:15.73
21	William Slider	Brown	2001	19:46.10
22	Jamal Bacon	Shawnee	2006	19:51.00
23	Eric Jeter	Brown	2004	19:51.30
24	William Slider	Brown	2004	19:58.69
25	William Slider	Brown	2004	19:59.37
26	William Slider	Brown	2003	19:59.89
27	Jamal Bacon	Shawnee	2006	20:00.61
28	Eric Jeter	Brown	2003	20:06.15
29	William Slider	Brown	2004	20:10.19
30	William Slider	Brown	2002	20:11.00
31	William Slider	Brown	2002	20:17.00
32	William Slider	Brown	2003	20:19.06
33	William Slider	Brown	2004	20:20.00
34	William Slider	Brown	2004	20:21.00
35	Eric Jeter	Brown	2004	20:21.00
36	William Slider	Brown	2004	20:21.08
37	Lee Bryant	Shawnee	2006	20:26.79
38	William Slider	Brown	2002	20:27.81
39	Tim Blunk	Brown	2003	20:29.78
40	Tim Blunk	Brown	2005	20:30.00

Top Ten Girls 4K Times

The girls rarely ran the 4 Kilometer distance. It was primarily a High School Junior Varsity and the Middle School State Championship distance.

Rank	Runner	School	Year	Time
1	Kelly McRoberts	Brown	2004	16:30.15
2	Kelly McRoberts	Brown	2003	17:22.25
3	Maddie Dailey	Brown	2004	18:24.00
4	Maddie Dailey	Brown	2004	18:35.37
5	Maddie Dailey	Brown	2003	19:41.37
6	Sami Siegwald	Brown	2004	20:00.00
7	Sami Siegwald	Brown	2003	20:20.33
8	Sami Siegwald	Brown	2005	21:50.97
9	Kayla Hill	Brown	2005	22:10.90
10	Erica Stoddard	Brown	2003	23:01.85

Top Twenty Boys 4K Times

I coached more boys; and therefore, had more opportunity to form Junior Varsity and Middle School teams to run the 4 Kilometer distance.

Rank	Runner	School	Year	Time
1	Eric Jeter	Brown	2004	14:46.23
2	William Slider	Brown	2002	15:15.00
3	Eric Jeter	Brown	2004	15:15.40
4	Clay McRoberts	Brown	2005	16:02.85
5	Tim Blunk	Brown	2004	16:03.00
6	Tim Blunk	Brown	2005	16:07.37
7	Isaac Poole	Brown	2005	16:08.04
8	Eric Jeter	Brown	2003	16:15.13
9	Josh Chervenak	Brown	2004	16:30.00
10	William Slider	Brown	2001	16:43.00
11	Blake Braden	Brown	2002	16:51.00
12	Jordan Smith	Brown	2004	16:59.00
13	Zach Torp	Brown	2004	17:04.00
14	David Read	Brown	2004	17:08.01
15	Isaac Poole	Brown	2004	17:08.80
16	Clay McRoberts	Brown	2005	17:22.30
17	Isaac Poole	Brown	2004	17:28.00
18	David Read	Brown	2003	17:28.29
19	Griffith Williams	Brown	2005	17:36.92
20	Isaac Poole	Brown	2005	17:38.90

Top Five Girls 3K Times

The 3 Kilometer distance was rarely run. It was the distance for the Elementary State Championship and a High School Varsity relay event that we ran a couple of years.

Rank	Runner	School	Year	Time
1	Kelly McRoberts	Brown	2004	12:02.00
2	Maddie Dailey	Brown	2004	12:58.00
3	Sami Siegwald	Brown	2004	14:19.00
4	Meagan Geary	Brown	2001	17:04.90
5	Ayanna Jeter	Brown	2004	17:30.08

Top Ten Boys 3K Times

Most of the boys I coached responded well to the 3 Kilometer distance.

Rank	Runner	School	Year	Time
1	Eric Jeter	Brown	2004	10:44.00
2	William Slider	Brown	2004	10:56.00
3	Tim Blunk	Brown	2004	11:21.00
4	Josh Chervenak	Brown	2004	11:48.00
5	Clay McRoberts	Brown	2004	11:49.00
6	Isaac Poole	Brown	2004	11:51.00
7	Griffith Williams	Brown	2004	12:18.00
8	Clay McRoberts	Brown	2004	12:31.86
9	Eric Jeter	Brown	2001	12:55.30
10	David Read	Brown	2004	13:07.00

The J. Graham Brown School Varsity Numbers

At the Brown School I awarded a singlet with a number on the back for an athlete to wear in his first varsity competition. These numbers were earned. Many meet officials appreciated these number because in larger meets it the Brown runner could be identified for finish place. Varsity numbers are considered to be assigned for life.

Number	Runner – Girl	Class
#1	Krysta Lathon	Class of 2010
#2	Kelly McRoberts	Class of 2009
#3	Maddie Dailey	Class of 2009
#4	Sami Siegwald	Class of 2010
#5	Erica Stoddard	Class of 2010
#6	Kayla Hill	Class of 2011

Number	Runner – Boys	Class
#1	Rob Halsell	Class of 2004
#2	William Slider	Class of 2005
#3	Scott Roser	Class of 2005
#4	Josh Chervenak	Class of 2006
#5	Blake Braden	Class of 2007
#6	Aaron Ray	Class of 2007
#7	Max Joslyn	Class of 2007
#8	Tim Blunk	Class of 2008
#9	Nick Logsdon	Class of 2008
#10	Brian Valentine	Class of 2008
#11	Eric Jeter	Class of 2009
#12	David Read	Class of 2009

#13	Zach Torp	Class of 2009
#14	Jordan Smith	Class of 2009
#15	Isaac Poole	Class of 2010
#16	Clay McRoberts	Class of 2012
#17	Griffith Brydon-Williams	Class of 2010
#18	Shelby Dixon	Class of 2010
#19	Jay Connelly	Class of 2010
#20	Houston Ward	Class of 2011
#21	Rhys Brydon-Williams	Class of 2010
#22	Zach Dettlinger	Class of 2010
#23	Alex Haynes	Class of 2011
#24	Gavin Curry	Class of 2013

J. Graham Brown School Cross Country Records

Very little information was passed on to me about the school records at either Brown School or Shawnee High School. I was able to establish some sense of the history of Cross Country at Brown and therefore developed a list of school records there.

Brown School Girls Records

Level[148]	Distance	Runner and Year	Time
Elementary	½ Mile	Krysta Lathon, 2002	3:07.00
Elementary	1 Mile	Krysta Lathon, 2002	7:50.00
Elementary	2K	Krysta Lathon, 2002	8:33.00
Elementary	3K	Meagan Geary, 2001	16:59.00
Middle School	½ Mile	Tia Stokes, 1995	2:48.00
Middle School	1 Mile	Kelly McRoberts, 2003	5:35.00
Middle School	2K	Kelly McRoberts, 2003	7:49.00
Middle School	3K	Sami Siegwald, 2003	14:30.80
Middle School	4K	Kelly McRoberts, 2004	16:30.15
Freshman	4K	Kayla Hill, 2005	22:10.09
Junior Varsity	4K	Kelly McRoberts, 2003	16:30.00
Varsity	3K	Kelly McRoberts, 2003	11:59.60
Varsity	5K	Kelly McRoberts, 2003	20:32.48
Varsity	3x3K	McRoberts, Dailey, Siegwald, 2004	39:19.90

[148] Elementary is considered 6th grade and under. Middle School is 7th and 8th grade. Junior Varsity is any race designated as JV or Reserve. A new category of "Freshman" has been established. Freshman is any time run in a Freshman race. Varsity is any varsity race.

Brown School Boys Records

Level	Distance	Runner and Year	Time
Elementary	½ Mile	Eric Jeter, 2001	2:50.00
Elementary	1 Mile	Eric Jeter, 2001	5:48.00
Elementary	2K	Eric Jeter, 2001	8:14.00
Elementary	3K	Clay McRoberts, 2004	11:49.00
Middle School	½ Mile	Maurice Ponder, 1988	2:25.00
Middle School	1 Mile	Eric Jeter, 2004	5:14.00
Middle School	2K	Price Matthews, 2001	7:29.00
Middle School	3K	Price Matthews, 2001	13:06.00
Middle School	4K	Eric Jeter, 2004	14:46.23
Freshman	4K	Clay McRoberts, 2005	17:22.30
Freshman	5K	Clay McRoberts, 2005	22:18.00
Junior Varsity	4K	William Slider, 2002; Eric Jeter, 2004	15:15.40
Junior Varsity	5K	William Slider, 2002	19:43.00
Varsity	3K	Rob Halsell, 2003	9:50.00
Varsity	4K	Rob Halsell, 2000	14:48.00
Varsity	5K	Rob Halsell, 2002	16:40.00
Varsity	3x3K	Blunk, Jeter, Slider, 2004	33:01.10

Coach Slider All-Time Cross Country Team

Position	Runner-Boy	Runner-Girl
Captain	Rob Halsell	Kelly McRoberts
#2	William Slider	Maddie Dailey
#3	Jamal Bacon	Krysta Lathon
#4	Eric Jeter	Sami Siegwald
#5	Lee Bryant	Erica Stoddard
#6	Tim Blunk	Kayla Hill
#7	Clay McRoberts	Mary Goode
Alternate	Josh Chervenak	Chelsae Lathon
Alternate	Isaac Poole	Erica Stoddard

Individual Awards

- Regional Champion – Rob Halsell (2003); Kelly McRoberts (2004)
- State Sportsmanship Award – Rob Halsell (2003)

- All-County-Academic – William Slider (2001, 2002, 2003, 2004); Tim Blunk (2002, 2003, 2004, 2005); Eric Jeter (2001, 2002, 2003, 2004); David Read (2003, 2004); Zach Torp (2003, 2004); Jordan Smith (2003, 2004); Isaac Poole (2004. 2005); Clay McRoberts (2004, 2005); Griffith Williams (2004, 2005); Rhys Williams (2005); Shelby Dixon (2005); Jay Connelly (2005); Krysta Lathon (2002, 2003); Kelly McRoberts (2003, 2004); Maddie Dailey (2003, 2004); Sami Siegwald (2003, 2004); Kayla Hill (2005); Jordan Klunk (2006); Lee Bryant (2006); Mary Goode (2006)

- All-State Academic – William Slider (2004); Tim Blunk (2004); Eric Jeter (2004); David Read (2004); Zach Torp (2004); Clay McRoberts (2004); Krysta Lathon (2002, 2003); Kelly McRoberts (2003, 2004); Maddie Dailey (2003, 2004)

- All-County – Rob Halsell (2001, 2002, 2003); William Slider (2003, 2004); Eric Jeter (2004); Clay McRoberts (2004, 2005); Kelly McRoberts (2003-2004)

- All-Conference – Rob Halsell (2003); Kelly McRoberts (2003, 2004)

- All-Regional – Rob Halsell (2001, 2002, 2003); Kelly McRoberts (2003, 2004)

- All-State – Rob Halsell (2003); Kelly McRoberts (2004)

- State Sportsmanship Award – Rob Halsell (2003)

- All-American[149] – William Slider (2004)

- AAU National Championship runners – William Slider (2004); Clay McRoberts (2004); Kelly McRoberts (2004); Maddie Dailey (2004)

Where Are They Now?

Several athletes that I coached went on to participate in college athletics. The following is a list to the best of my knowledge of the students I coached, and the sports in which they participated.

---

[149] William Slider received All-American Second Team recognition from Athletes of Good News. He was honored for his accomplishments in Cross Country, Swimming, and Track and for his academic achievements and Christian service. William also received recognition as a Scholastic All-American and on the National High School Sports Honor Roll. He has been listed in Who's Who in High School Sports.

Runner	School	Class	College	Sports	Level	Scholarship
Rob Halsell	Brown	2004	Eastern Kentucky	XC, Track	NCAA D1	XC, Track
William Slider	Brown	2005	Univ. of the Cumberlands	Swimming, XC	NAIA	XC, Swimming
Jamal Bacon	Shawnee	2007	Spalding University	Basketball, XC	NAIA	Basketball
Eric Jeter	Brown	2009	N. Kentucky University	XC	NCAA D2	XC
Kelly McRoberts	Brown	2009	Hanover College	Soccer	NCAA D3	150
Austin Pegram	Brown	2009	Centre College	Soccer	NCAA D3	
Zach Torp	Brown	2009	University of Louisville	Soccer	NCAA D1	Soccer
Shelby Dixon	Brown	2010	Transylvania University	Baseball	NAIA	Baseball

---

150 NCAA D3 does not provide athletic scholarships.

18 PHOTOGRAPHS

The 2004 Brown School Cross Country team at the Class A State Championships in Lexington, Kentucky: (from left to right) David Read, Clay McRoberts, Josh Chervenak, Tim Blunk, Coach John Slider, Maddie Dailey, Eric Jeter, Alum Rob Halsell, Zach Torp, Captain William Slider, Kelly McRoberts, and Isaac Poole.

The 2004 Brown School Cross Country Team at the Class A Region 2 Championships. All runners qualified for the Class A State Championship: (from left to right standing) Coach John Slider, Isaac Poole, Captain William Slider, Josh Chervenak, Zach Torp, Tim Blunk, David Read, Kelly McRoberts (Girls Individual Champion), Eric Jeter; (kneeling left to right (Clay McRoberts and Maddie Dailey. Photograph taken after the girls race and before the boys race by Phil Blunk,

Mile 2 at Creason Park

Rob Halsell (front row center) and William Slider (front row right) with their teammates and coach. This team was the 13/14 Mason-Dixon Athletic Club boys team that finished 10th at the 2000 AAU national championship.

Made in the USA
Lexington, KY
10 November 2012